SOMETHING REALLY NEW

SOMETHING REALLY NEW:

Three Simple Steps to Creating Truly Innovative Products

Denis J. Hauptly

AMACOM

AMERICAN MANAGEMENT ASSOCIATION

New York · Atlanta · Brussels · Chicago · Mexico City
San Francisco · Shanghai · Tokyo · Toronto · Washington, D.C.

This publication is designed to provide accurate and authoritative information in regard to the subject matter covered. It is sold with the understanding that the publisher is not engaged in rendering legal, accounting, or other professional service. If legal advice or other expert assistance is required, the services of a competent professional person should be sought.

Library of Congress Cataloging-in-Publication Data

Hauptly, Denis J.
   Something really new : three simple steps to creating truly innovative products / Denis J. Hauptly.
     p. cm.
   Includes bibliographical references and index.
   ISBN 978-0-8144-0032-6 (hardcover)
   1. New products.   2. Product management.   I. Title.
HF5415.153.H38   2008
658.5'75—dc22

2007033586

Printing number

10 9 8 7 6 5 4 3 2 1

As the song goes:

> *"That book would be like my heart and me, dedicated to you."*

And so it is.

Contents

Acknowledgments

THIS BOOK IS DERIVED FROM EXPERIENCES IN AND OBSERVA-
tions of a series of very large organizations and working with
"products" that varied from software applications to educa-
tional seminars to criminal codes. There is more in common
among these things than one might expect. Bureaucracies are
the same in every context. All very large organizations have
many able people and some deadwood as well. Of course,
each organization was unique in some ways, but one thing
that all of these experiences had in common was the opportunity to work with very talented people in cultures that cher-
ished innovation. This book could not be long enough to
acknowledge all of the people in those organizations who
helped develop my thinking on innovation.

With respect to the development of this book, though, it

is possible to express particular gratitude toward those who have spent real time to help advance the project. In particular, I would like to express my appreciation to Shelly Albaum, whose lengthy and, as always, insightful comments illustrate once more why he is my avatar of innovators; David Hanssens, who took the time to read and comment on the manuscript while recovering from his 50th birthday celebration; Martin Hyndman, whose own insistence on a clear understanding of user requirements serves as an object lesson in applying the principles in the book; Peter Jackson, who steered me into parallel analyses that have greatly advanced my thinking; Kay Knapp, who spent countless hours reading and rereading and adding both nuance and precision to the book; and Chris Morton, who, in addition to always referring to me as "sir" and strongly encouraging the project from the outset, also insisted that the method I was proposing applied just as well to service businesses as it did to hard and soft products.

I would also like to express my appreciation to my agent, John Willig, for not only steering the book rapidly to publication, but doing so with grace.

I have left off a few hundred people who deserve some sort of recognition here, but I hope they will all attribute that to my constantly failing memory, and not to a lack of appreciation.

SOMETHING REALLY NEW

Let's Get Started

Every innovation has a special moment. There comes a brief flash when you recognize that you have crossed some barrier, gained some significant new insight, or developed some new paradigm. This story involves one of those moments, and it sets the stage for much of what is to follow in this book.

In the late 1980s, I was part of a group of government officials and judges from the United States who had been asked to spend several days in discussions with policy officials from the Italian judiciary in Rome. It was at a time when there had been several terrorist attacks in Italy, and I have vivid recollections of being picked up at the airport and driven to my hotel in what amounted to an armored car, and eating dinner in a private room at a restaurant guarded by several serious-looking fellows with armored vests and Uzis.

The purpose of our visit was interesting. Italy, like most European nations, had a criminal justice system that was quite different from that of the United States. The lead investigator in a case was essentially the judge as well. He would take the lead in directing the police to collect evidence against someone and then would also lead the trial.

This system is not as draconian as it may seem. The investigating judge is theoretically neutral and gathers evidence favorable to the defense as well. In practice, however, it is hard to be entirely neutral when you are pursuing someone who you come to believe has committed a serious crime.

The system had recently been changed by the legislature to something more like the system that Americans are used to: Prosecutors would gather evidence and present it to a judge who had not been involved in the investigation. My colleagues and I were there to advise our counterparts on what this change might mean and what steps they should take to prepare for it.

The meeting was held in a large nineteenth-century room with 30 or more people seated in a square. We spoke in English, which was translated into Italian, and so matters moved along slowly. I focused some of my discussion on the issue of abuse of prosecutorial discretion. Under the old system, I assumed, this had not been an issue in Italy. The prosecutor, after all, was a judge—a neutral figure, not an advocate. Thus, the decision to charge a person with a crime was a judicial act. Judges did not abuse their discretion, or so the theory went.

In the course of my discussion, I realized from puzzled

looks and whispered conversations that the audience was confused by my remarks. I stopped and asked what the problem was. It took several questions and translations to get to the nub of the issue.

My audience understood the notion of abuse of prosecutorial discretion perfectly. Contrary to my assumption, it had worried them quite a bit under the old system. But it meant something very different to them from what it did to me. When the difference, and the reason for the confusion, became clear, there were several gasps in the room.

To my audience, abuse of prosecutorial discretion meant failing to file charges when charges were justified. To me, it meant filing charges for some improper motive—personal animus or racial bias or the like. In my world, their concern was very far-fetched. In their world, the problem I was presenting was unimaginable.

So what has all this talk of arcane criminal law issues in Italy two decades ago got to do with product[1] innovation in business in the twenty-first century in America? Quite a bit, I think.

What happened in that frescoed room 20 years ago happened because I and they both were products of the culture we grew up in. Those cultures predisposed us to look at the world in a certain way. The more deeply we got involved in our culture, the more difficult it was for us to escape its gravitational pull. The more bounded we were by our own frame of reference, the more difficult it became not simply to understand another frame of reference, but to imagine it at all.

Within our frame of reference, we could be effective and could even be change agents, but only within our frame of reference. We could not be truly innovative because we could not see beyond our frame of reference. We could not think outside the box. However, the moment we all realized that we were operating with different frames of reference, we were able to shift to a common one and to propose truly innovative solutions.

I have used this story many times since (I am told that I repeat most of my stories many times) to illustrate the power of culture to interfere with communication. But it has another lesson as well. The Italians were my customers. I was being rewarded (with an all-expenses-paid trip to Rome) for giving them information that was useful to them. However, because I did not understand their context properly, I spent quite a bit of time discussing a topic that was of no value to them at all.

Perhaps I am being a bit harsh on myself. Didn't the Italians have some responsibility for communicating that context to me? Shouldn't they have understood their own problem and asked me relevant questions based on that understanding?

The answer to these questions is no. They were buying, and I was selling. It was my job to understand their needs, not their job to define those needs for me in unambiguous terms.

Anyone who has ever used focus groups, surveys, or other forms of market research knows what I am talking about. If we ask people what they want in a product or show them a concept and seek their reaction, we run a very high risk of failure if we take their responses literally.

In another life, designing software, I would present an idea to focus groups, and I would be tickled pink to see their positive reactions, the exclamations of "That's cool!" and the like. Then we would add a feature based on this positive input and find that it was never used. We had asked, "Do you like this?" That's the wrong question. People always like stuff that is cool, and it is very easy to be cool in a PowerPoint presentation on a proposed piece of software. Whether people like an idea or not is irrelevant. What we need to know is, will they buy it and, having bought it, will they use it? Does the customer find this feature both valuable in theory and useful in practice?

Before we can rely on the answers we get, we have to be sure that we are asking the right questions. Very often we are not, because our frame of reference is very different from that of the people answering the questions and because we are asking questions that we *want* to hear the answer to, not questions that we *need* to hear the answer to.

If we can ask the right questions, we will have a very powerful, very relevant response. If we fail to do so, we will march with great confidence and full speed down precisely the wrong road.

This book has one guiding thesis: It takes the perspective that in the world of product and service innovation, utility is the driving force. That statement is important because it embodies the assumptions on which this book is built. So let us go through this concept and see whether these assumptions hold up.

People buy something for one of two reasons: because it

is beautiful, or because it is useful. We buy things only for either aesthetic reasons or utilitarian reasons. Please be cynical about that statement. Go through your own purchases in the recent past, and look for something that does not fit into one of those two boxes. Remember, we are talking about goods and services here. Contributing to a charity is not a purchase of goods or a use of services.

How about CDs or DVDs? Well, music is beautiful and film is beautiful (or at least entertaining—a variation on aesthetic pleasure). What about paint? We do not buy paint for our living room that we find repulsive. We buy a color that we think is beautiful. Food? Nothing is more useful than staying alive.

I would be very surprised if you can come up with a third category.

If utility and beauty are the reasons why we buy things, then innovation must be responsive to one or the other. It must represent either a new form of beauty or a notable advance in utility.

This statement seems obvious, and our first instinct is to say that product development efforts must always have been guided by these concepts. But that is not true. Think about two words: Pet Rock. Then about three more: voice transcription software. Both of these developments represent a false third category: novelty. You buy a Pet Rock because it is amusing in concept, and therefore apparently beautiful. But it turned out that Pet Rocks were neither useful nor beautiful. Of the millions of Pet Rocks sold in the 1960s and 1970s, there are probably very few still gracing the family rooms of

America—and even the few that remain are probably there as monuments to nostalgia.

Voice transcription software appears to have great utility. Typing without typing! Who can resist that concept? Unfortunately, at least to date, the promise has not been achieved. In my experience, it takes more effort to write with voice transcription software than it does to type.

But people buy things like Pet Rocks and voice transcription software, don't they? Yes, they do. But, like those who respond to Nigerian oil e-mails, they do it only once. When people discover that these products have neither beauty nor utility, the market for them dries up.

In this book, we are not concerned about beauty. Our focus is not on art or music or decoration. It is on products that are not aesthetic and on services.[2] So the right questions here have to do with utility. They need to let us understand usefulness and create product innovations that enhance usefulness. At some level, everyone involved in product development understands that (although the number of merely "cool" products that make it to the market is amazing).

This book will take you through a process involving three steps. Those steps are presented in the form of questions. Those three questions, which will be revealed and discussed in detail in later chapters, are aimed at finding where the customer is expending resources unnecessarily and innovating by reducing those inefficiencies. It is a simple and straightforward process, and one that will enable you to quickly and inexpensively create new product and service innovations that have real value to customers.

Each step builds upon the answer to the previous question. The first step is foundational. It establishes our baseline. The second step takes the answer to the first question and shows how to apply it simply and effectively in the real world. Genuine innovation follows directly from the answers to the second question. The third step moves us from an individual product or service to workflow and thus presents opportunities to enhance customer loyalty and to enter entirely new product areas.

Most of the discussion and examples in the first part of the book focus on "hard" product innovation. The penultimate chapter in this part discusses the special case of innovation in the services industry, and the final chapter summarizes the method that has been put forth.

These steps can lead your company to the ideas it needs if it is to grow. But that will not happen automatically. Asking the right questions is necessary but not sufficient for innovation to take place. So the second part of the book discusses finding the right people. Innovators are different from other people in some ways. And some innovators have plenty of new ideas, but absolutely no judgment as to which are good and which are bad. Getting the right mix of what I will call pragmatic innovators and these ultra-innovators will be a primary task here.

We also discuss how to optimize the organization for innovation. This too is tricky and is likely to disrupt existing fiefdoms, but the rewards are significant.

Chapter 12 demonstrates that the three steps are not just a tool for developing product concepts. They can also be used by top management to help determine what projects should be approved and what projects should be sent back to the drawing board.

Before we dive into the first step, let us examine a basic assumption of this book: that innovation matters, because if it does not matter, we can stop right here.

PART 1

Three Simple Steps to Innovation

Chapter 1

Money Is the Root of All Innovation

You PROBABLY WOULD NOT BE READING THIS BOOK IF YOU didn't think innovation mattered to your business. But it will still be useful to spend just a couple of pages reviewing the question of *why* it matters, because changing your approach to innovation is a major decision, and there needs to be a clear justification for doing so.

Let me clarify. Some of the methods in this book are very simple to apply. Indeed, you are probably applying some of them now. But others are more difficult. For most organizations, optimizing staffing and organization for innovation requires a real commitment to change. In order to consider such change, there has to be a great deal to gain. I believe that there is.

Innovation and the Bottom Line

In 2006, *BusinessWeek* did a survey on innovation. It compiled a list of the top 25 innovative companies in the world. Then it compared the results of those companies with those of their peers in the S&P Global 1200. The median profit margin growth for the innovative companies was 3.4 percent per year from 1995 to 2005. The median growth for the rest of the S&P group was 0.4 percent over the same period of time. Similarly, the median annual stock return was 14.3 percent for the innovators and 11.3 percent for the rest.[1]

A *Harvard Business Review* article in 1997 examined the numbers more granularly. It divided innovations into Incremental and Next Generation innovations. Incremental innovations accounted for 86 percent of product launches, 62 percent of revenue from innovations, and 39 percent of profit from innovations. Next Generation innovations represented 14 percent of launches, 38 percent of revenue, and a whopping 61 percent of profits from product innovations.[2]

Those numbers are impressive. Innovation drives top-line growth, and it delivers bottom-line growth as well, if done effectively. Procter & Gamble, perennially one of the top innovative companies, reports that a new innovation program doubled the success rate of its new innovations (as measured against their business cases), while R&D investment as a percentage of sales dropped from 4.8 percent to 3.4 percent.[3]

So getting innovation right is a keystone of business success. It is not the only route. Marketing is another route to such achievement. But marketing can do only so much by itself. Ultimately, you cannot continually market bad products, although there are companies that try to do just that. For marketing to succeed, innovation must succeed first. A company must have something more to offer than its management.

Take a look at your marketing budget and compare it to your innovation budget. The odds are pretty good that you are spending multiples of the innovation budget on the marketing budget. That will always be the case, of course. Getting the word out and getting it out well are difficult and expensive tasks. But those tasks are made easier (and less expensive) if the product being marketed is genuinely innovative. More investment in innovation can lead to less need for marketing or higher returns on marketing dollars. Either way, you win.

Let us take a closer look at this concept. Products exist on a continuum. At one end, we have a pure commodity—we'll use water as an example. At the other end, we have products that are truly cutting edge—the first of their breed. Here we will use the new (and disputed) weight loss drinks.

At the commodity end, we have a product, water, that, at first glance, is indistinguishable from any other water, with competition being based on price. But if we add a little marketing magic to it—brand it with a catchy brand name, associate it in advertising with youthfulness and good health—and pretty soon we have created a premium level of the commodity and can price it higher than the competition.

Then suppose we add some lime flavor to it and jack the price up another dime. Now we throw in some magic herbs and spices and call it an "energy drink." Suddenly we are in a new category where we are no longer selling water and the old pricing rules do not apply. When that category becomes a commodity, we can shift the emphasis from staying awake to the even more popular idea of staying slim. Again, we have a new category.

Each step along the continuum after premium branding involved an innovation of sorts. Each innovation took the product further from commodity pricing and allowed the same marketing dollars to be spent on a product with larger margins. Innovation jump-started the drive to higher revenue and greater profits.

Innovation and Customer Perception

Innovation matters in customer perception as well. If you have an image as a company that does not innovate, customers will be less likely to look at your new products. We expect innovation from 3M, and so we look for it when we see a 3M product. We do not expect innovation from Sears (rightly or wrongly). Its brand is associated with reliable basic value. If 3M announces a new innovation, we are likely to pay close attention. If Sears did, we might not read the story.

This perception goes far beyond the initial buying decision. Apple made a huge hit with the iPod. Its stock went up 600 percent in a few years. But something else happened as well. In the fourth quarter of 2005, Apple reported that it had shipped 1,254,000 Macintosh computers, and that that represented 20 percent growth in Macs over the same quarter a year earlier. The 207 percent growth in iPods during that same quarter had a halo effect on Apple computers, leading to 20 percent growth in a fairly stagnant computer hardware market. That growth came out of other people's market share, and it came in spite of the fact that Apple had announced but not yet introduced its Intel-powered Macs, which many consumers were waiting for.[4]

Consumers loved the iPod. Because they loved the iPod, they loved Apple. Because they loved Apple, they broke away from the "Wintel" computers and tried out a Mac. Every satisfied iPod customer became a potential Mac customer. This tendency was helped greatly by the fact that lots of iPods were sold out of Apple stores, where the consumer buying an iPod came face to face with a whole gaggle of cleverly designed, lustrous white Apple products. But those customers who walked out with Macs often had walked in to buy an iPod.

And even those who did not leave with a Mac left with a device that greatly facilitated and rewarded their use of a new way of buying music—the iTunes Music Store. Sales of CDs dropped 4 percent in the first half of 2006 alone, while iTunes sold a billion digital songs that year. One industry leader predicts that online sales will grow 25 percent this year and that the day of the CD is passing quickly.[5] The iPod created a huge market for itself, a dependent market in iTunes, and a halo-effect market for Macs. It does not get better than that.

There is one more good reason to put more focus on innovation: Innovation energizes a business. You can launch a new marketing campaign for an old product and boost sales for a period, but you do not generate organizational excitement that way. Launch a new product that people believe is a winner and the marketing people get energized, the salespeople get energized, and even the finance people get energized. That enthusiasm provides the energy that makes each component do a better job than it might otherwise have done. And that energy carries the organization forward. Success breeds success, and innovation in product breeds innovation in marketing, sales, and even business model.

Can these things happen without innovation? Maybe, although keeping sales and marketing motivated when they have no good new products to bring to the market is a serious struggle. But motivation is a natural product of innovation that is itself good for the business.

In the end, this comes down to something very simple. Innovation matters because people buy two things: commodities and innovations. For the former, they pay the lowest price they can find, and for the latter, they pay a premium. Which type of business do you want to be in?

Chapter 2

Step 1: Fixing the Faucet

STEP 1 ASKS THE MOST IMPORTANT QUESTION, SO WE SHALL spend a good deal of time on this step. But it represents a concept that is neither complex nor hard to implement in the end. It is a concept that arises in every form of business that has a "product." The problem is that this concept very often gets lost when the day-to-day demands of operations dominate time and thinking.

Fixing Faucets

Our quest begins in the kitchen of an ordinary house—your house. That kitchen has a sink in it, and the sink has a faucet.

That faucet has many attributes. It may be chrome or gold or bronze or white or any of several other colors. It may have two handles (one each for hot and cold), or it may have just one handle that swivels and lifts to adjust temperature and water pressure. It may be part of a set of devices that includes a spray head or a water purifier.

But, despite these variations, a faucet is a commodity. Right? Everybody has one. Actually, most Americans have many. In my two-bathroom house, I counted nine faucet sets. We don't change our faucets often. They rarely need repairs. Their style is dictated to some degree by their surroundings—gold faucet sets are unlikely to be found in a stainless steel kitchen. Within each of two general classes (separate hot and cold controls and blended hot and cold controls), they operate in pretty much the same way. Price differentiation takes place based on materials, design, and brand/quality values.

Growth in the plumbing fixtures industry has been steady but low—about 3 to 4 percent per year for the past decade. Growth comes from new construction and remodeling of existing houses.[1] Faucets last a long time and are easy to repair, so people rarely replace them outside the context of a remodeling.

But you are about to change that. You are about to turn the plumbing fixtures industry on its ear. You are going to create such an innovative product that everyone planning new construction will want to use it and existing homeowners will have a strong incentive to replace what they have now with your new product. Moreover, if you do this really well, you will even come up with new uses for the faucet. Growth rates will hit 6 or 7 percent, and prices and margins will increase. Your bonus will be staggering. Don't think fishing boat, think yacht.

But first you have to ask the right question. The good news is that this is not that hard to do. It is a lot more likely that you will find the right question than that you will find the winning lottery ticket.

The Faucet Problem

The faucet industry urgently needs to innovate.[2] The differentiation that comes from innovation is what allows this commodity product to maintain a premium price. You have just been thrown into this lion's den. Your boss, a curmudgeonly sort who has thrived as a commodity thinker and hasn't had a new idea in 11 years, has responded to pressure from above and made you the brand new Kitchen Product Development guru for Feisty Faucets. It is up to you to come up with some notions for next year's product line, to be introduced at the National Kitchen & Bath Trade Show. If you fail, you will be out, and the curmudgeon will have someone else to blame for his lack of innovation.

Here's some market research derived from the articles in footnotes 2 and 3 of Chapter 2 (and embellished a bit for ease of use) that may or may not be helpful to you.

When asked what motivated their buying decisions on kitchen faucets, purchasers listed the factors in this order:

1. Style/color
2. Durability/warranty
3. Price
4. Brand

When asked what they liked most about their current kitchen faucets, homeowners ranked their results in this order:

1. Style/color
2. Durability
3. Ease of repair

The emphases on style and durability have not been lost on manufacturers. The motto of Moen, a leading faucet maker, is "Buy for Looks—Buy for Life."[3] Delta's motto is "We Work Wonders with Water."[4] Moen and Delta each have about 25 percent of the market, and these two companies seem to have much the same philosophy.

So here is your task: Given what you now know about the kitchen faucet business, and given what you can easily find out by, say, walking into the kitchen and looking at a faucet, give yourself 10 minutes to come up with two good product innovations for kitchen faucets. There are no other rules. There are winners and losers, but you will be the only one to know which category you fall into.

GO

Now, we will assume that 10 minutes have gone by and that you have two ideas written down. See if you can find something like your idea in the following list. It doesn't have to match up exactly, just be pretty close.

1. Faucets with removable "skins" so that you can change the color whenever you want
2. Faucets with various wood tones
3. A retractable faucet that hides away when not in use
4. A "retro" faucet look
5. An ultrathin faucet handle that is virtually invisible
6. An easy-to-clean, crud-free faucet
7. An easy-to-replace faucet

Is your idea in that group or reasonably close to it? Well, then you lose. None of these are innovations. They are merely mutations. The difference between innovations and mutations is one that we will cover in depth in a later chapter, but for now the important thing is this: If your answer is like the ones on this list, then you failed to ask a basic question. You were lured away from innovating by market research that simply reflects a similar failure to ask the right question. The folks who did that research accepted the idea that faucets were a commodity, and thus they felt that differentiation would be based on style—on which faucet was prettiest.

That is nonsense, because "prettiness" is as much a commodity in faucets as it is in beauty contests. You have to have prettiness, but so does everyone else. Any faucet can be made pretty. Consumers will go for the prettiest faucet, but that is an entirely subjective judgment. It splinters the product into a hundred styles. Then those styles compete for market share.

All these "innovations" do is commoditize the product further by commoditizing the dimension "pretty." In the end, your product does not stand out from the rest in any meaningful way. The 5 percent of purchasers who think your product is prettiest will buy it, but the 95 percent who prefer some other style will not. You have forced yourself into a niche because you have focused on a narrow aspect of the product.

Innovation, especially in what appears to be a commoditized product line, requires a quite different approach from merely changing the appearance of the faucet or the flavor of the cereal or the placement of the ice machine on the refrigerator door.

Getting Down to Tasks

As is so often the case, Bruce Springsteen may have said it best. In early 2006 he was interviewed about his forthcoming album featuring songs associated with Pete Seeger, the American folk singer. He explained the difficulty of covering a song that had long been famous and was deeply associated with the civil rights movement in the 1960s:

"When the idea came to do 'We Shall Overcome,' I was like, 'I can't do that,'" he said. "Everyone knows that song as an icon. But what was it before it became that? So I went back and looked and realized: 'Oh, this is a prayer. I can do that. I know how to pray.'"[5]

Applying that same approach of going back to basics, we seek to answer this question in Step 1:

What tasks is the product really used for?

Well, that's a relatively simple question to answer, isn't it? It is—if you understand the difference between task and function. The function of all faucets is to provide access to flowing water. That's true for the faucet in the kitchen, the one in the bathroom sink, the one in the tub or shower, and the one outside in the garden. The function tells us what a faucet does, not what tasks it is intended to facilitate. If we mistake function for task, then all we can do is change the color or style, and there is no innovation in that because it does not facilitate the task. It does not make the faucet better at doing the thing we use it for.

To innovate, we must get beyond functions and understand the tasks. And tasks differ, even for faucets.

In the bathroom sink, my tasks are:
• Wash hands.
• Obtain drinking water.
• Brush teeth.

In the tub, my tasks are:
• Fill tub.
• Rinse hair.

In the garden, my tasks are:
• Provide water for plants and grass.
• Clean outside surfaces.

In the kitchen, my tasks are:
- Wash hands.
- Wash dishes.
- Wash food.
- Obtain specific amounts of water for cooking.

Now we are on to something. We are no longer dealing with abstract faucets. We are dealing with faucets in a context, and that context includes specific tasks. These tasks can be analyzed, and we can see how well the kitchen faucet performs each of them. It turns out that the kitchen faucet does a pretty poor job at what it is supposed to do. It turns out that this "commodity" has acres of room for innovation. Each faucet location has different tasks associated with it, so having a single faucet design is itself wrong. But that is essentially what the plumbing fixtures industry has provided. Faucets in all locations are essentially the same except for style, even though they are intended to do quite different things. Each location would clearly benefit from a different design. For instance, a garden faucet can benefit from a built-in easy hose connection. In fact, a proprietary hose connection for a garden faucet that was really good would allow you to gain a piece of the hose market as well because you would build the compatible hose. That same easy hose connection would be useless in the bathroom sink.

Let us take a closer look at three of the tasks associated with our kitchen faucet:

Task 1: Wash hands.
Task 2: Wash dishes.
Task 3: Wash food.

What could be simpler than washing one's hands? We have been doing it all our lives, and it is very simple to do. First, you go to the sink. Second, you obtain a soap of some sort, which, one hopes, is located near the sink. Third, you turn on the water and set it to a temperature that is warm but still comfortable. Fourth, you wet your hands. Fifth, you apply the soap. Sixth, you rub your hands vigorously together to clean them. Seventh, you rinse your hands under the still running water. Eighth, you dry your hands on a nearby towel. Ninth, you turn off the water.

Why, it's as easy as 1, 2, 3 . . . 4, 5, 6, 7, 8, 9.

But, seriously, it has taken you nine steps, and you have poured a couple of gallons of heated water down the drain. You have engaged in an activity that is a lot more complicated than it needs to be, and you have wasted water and energy at the same time. And, in truth, you have defeated your own purpose because your ninth step was to touch the faucet again—a faucet that was last touched by your dirty hands. "There must be a better way to do this," you say. Well, there is.

The great hand washers of the world are doctors. They wash their hands constantly and efficiently. Their sinks have a foot pedal that allows them to start the flow of water at a preset temperature and to stop it without using their hands. They achieve the same result as the nine-step method with greater simplicity and much less waste of water and energy. Similar advances have been adopted at many public restrooms, where sensor-activated faucets start the flow of water at a preset temperature.

That's innovation. And this same innovation both simplifies and makes more efficient the tasks of washing dishes and washing food. Go to your local Home Depot and see if you find this option in the kitchen faucet section.

Of course, such faucets are manufactured now. We see them in doctors' offices and restaurant kitchens. You can buy them from plumbing supply stores. But you would be hard pressed to find them in the largest faucet market of all—the home market.

Now let us look at the fourth kitchen faucet task: Obtain specific amounts of water for cooking.

Our foot-pedal kitchen faucet would make this task easier as well, but there are two other innovations that would make this task simpler still. First, as we analyze the task, we see that water is usually measured in cups or in fluid ounces, which are readily convertible to cups. What if we could just put a pot under a faucet, hit a button one time for each cup we wanted, and then leave while premeasured amounts of water flowed from the faucet? That would certainly make life simpler and would remove the need to get out a measuring device as well. It would also save water and energy because we wouldn't have water flowing while we moved the measuring cup from the faucet to the pot. And then we would not have to clean a measuring cup.

But even better, what if such a measuring faucet was located not at the sink, but on the stove itself? If the amount is premeasured and there is no risk of overflow, then you do not need to use the sink to get the water you need for cooking. You can save steps as well as energy and water. And your kitchen is more useful as well. How many times in a one-sink kitchen have you waited to get water from the sink faucet while the sink was being used for something else?

Finding the Task Underneath the Function

The types of innovations I have just described are not derived from understanding market research or from understanding how faucets work. They are derived from understanding the task. Knowing what the tasks are is the first step toward innovation. It is not the final step, but it is the essential step. After the tasks have been identified, then other steps are needed. Pain points must be identified, and aftermarket products (such as measuring cups, which are aftermarket products for faucets) must be looked at to see how they can be displaced. But you will get nowhere at all without looking at the tasks.

But, you say, good market research will reveal this. "You can find this out in focus groups." Probably not. Your average customers have the same problem you have in product development: They have a good deal of difficulty looking past the existing paradigm. They take as a given the fact that they have to use a cup to measure water and do not challenge it. They go into a Home Depot faucet department looking at color and style. They are not looking for a self-measuring faucet. You have to walk through a task and analyze each step before you come to this result. Market research is not likely to bring you there because the customer in the focus group or survey panel is unlikely to have gone through the analysis necessary for you to see what needs to be done.

As the innovator, your task is to go out and observe and know deeply the tasks that your products facilitate. You must understand hand washing (the task), not water flow (the function). Once you identify the tasks, then you can bring proposed innovations to focus groups and the like. If you have analyzed the tasks correctly, then you will see a response that includes a lot of "Wows." If you haven't analyzed the tasks correctly, you will hear a lot of "Huhs?" or "So whats?" instead.

If you do not hear "Wows," then you have not changed a thing. If you do hear "Wows," then some consumers will be motivated to buy new faucets even when they are not remodeling because the new faucets that you designed will help them complete their tasks so much more efficiently.

Let me give you a real-world example. In the mid-1990s, I was leading feature development for Westlaw, the online legal research system. Though the world of online was new to most Americans, Westlaw had already been online for 20 years and was a mature product with a large customer base. It was then in release 6.x.

We were moving the product from a software application that was loaded on your computer to one that would be found on the Internet through a browser. As part of that process, research was done to figure out what tasks people were actually using Westlaw for. The research was to be done by examining thousands of Westlaw sessions (without knowing who had done the sessions, of course) and seeing which functions were used together. With that information, we could readily surmise what tasks were involved.

Intuitively we knew the answer. Customers would conduct a search among the millions of legal cases on Westlaw. They would do this by entering some search terms and examining the 20 or more cases they got back as results. They would find a highly relevant case and then would use a tool in the software to determine whether that case was still good law and which cases had followed it. We knew that this would be what they were doing because we knew that Westlaw was really a gigantic index to a body of knowledge. After all, we had built it, and who would know better than we what it was used for?

Well, one group knew better than we: our customers. This was not the main task at all. It wasn't even close. The main task was to take the name of a known case (such as *Brown* v. *Board of Education*), enter that name in a special search template that would bring back that case and that case only, and then print it.

That was it.

The chief task that customers were using this enormously sophisticated application for was to avoid going down to the library and making a photocopy of a case. They were using it as a Xerox® machine.

But because we had been so focused on the powerful research functions and because we did not know what tasks the customers were actually doing, we had made this particular task very difficult to do.

A customer had to:

1. Open the software.
2. Sign in to the service.
3. Open up the template.
4. Enter the case citation.
5. Hit the Go button.
6. Wait for the case to be displayed on the screen.

7. Invoke the Print function.
8. Select the print format.
9. Select the printer.
10. Execute the final Print command.
11. If a second case was wanted, go back to Step 3.

We had taken the most useful task that the product performed from the customers' perspective and made the users go through 10 or 11 steps to get it done. And the task itself was actually very simple.

In response, we built a special tool called Find & Print. This was a simple web site that allowed users to enter up to ten case names at once, click one button, and get all of them printed by their local printers immediately. The number of steps was reduced from 11 to 4. Our customers were very happy. Not only had we saved them time, but we had allowed them to delegate the task as well. Generally only lawyers were trained to use Westlaw, but an administrative assistant or paralegal could be trained to use Find & Print in a few minutes.

The product achieved major revenue numbers in three years. It made it more likely that lawyers would use our product instead of the competition's product. And the lesson it taught stayed with every member of the development team forever. We had done a poor job for our customers because we had not gotten around to asking the right question:

What tasks is the product really used for?

From that point on, our analysis always included asking that basic question at the outset. Sometimes it would be phrased, "What will people do with this?" Sometimes, more formally, we would say, "But what is the use case?" In the end, though, it was all about the same thing.

Innovation Workouts

You probably have the general idea now. But it is always good to practice. One workout is provided here, but you will gain a great deal if you come up with some of your own. Workouts are all around you. Go to a store or an automobile repair shop. Go into Home Depot or Target and look at products and ask yourself: What tasks is this product really used for? You will find yourself doing this automatically fairly quickly, and each time you see a product or service that is not aligned with its task, then you will see an opportunity for innovation. Each time you see an opportunity for innovation, you will come up with some ideas that capitalize on that opportunity. Each time you do that, you will be training yourself to do more and better innovation. Pretty soon you will come to realize how much opportunity for innovation there really is and how much of that opportunity is wasted on novelty items or product line extensions.

One or more innovation workouts will be found at the end of each of the key chapters. In addition, Appendix B contains several more workouts with sample answers included. Doing these workouts is a core part of internalizing the method in this book, and they can also serve as a good focus for team development activities.

Innovation Workout 1: Opening a New Window

You are a manufacturer of windows. They come in a variety of sizes and styles, and some slide up and some open out. Some are wood and some are metal. Some are sold to people who live in cold climates, and some are sold to people who live in warm climates. Wherever they are used and whatever style they come in, window design has remained fairly constant. You can go to Mt. Vernon and see George Washington's windows and recognize them as essentially the same as yours. The main differences you will note will involve the inclusion of screens mounted on tracks in the window or attached to the outer part. I am sure President Washington would have liked these items, living as close to the Potomac River as he did, but they were not available. Your task here is to reexamine the household window. You should observe and see how real people use windows in their everyday lives in the twenty-first century and how they would like to use windows, but cannot because the product will not let them. For those real people, you can choose from among your friends and neighbors, or you can use the following person: Sam lives in Seattle, Washington. The climate there is temperate. It is not too hot and not very cold. There is an extended rainy season. Sam likes a cool house, especially at night. There are few mosquitoes in his area. He also has two cats that are indoor cats.

So this is the first of our three steps. We will get to the others shortly, but we need to look at a couple of other things first. For instance, completing Step 1 does not guarantee that you will respond to it correctly or optimally. You can ask the right question and come up with either the wrong answer or an answer that is correct but less than totally satisfactory. When you do so, you can waste a good deal of time and money before you discover your mistake. While *eventually* coming up with the right answer is better than *never* coming up with it, efficiency matters in business. So let us examine the subject of questions and answers and see if we can find a way to improve our odds of getting the best answers to the right questions.

Chapter 3

But First You Have to Ask the Right Question

ONE SUNDAY IN 2006, THE *NEW YORK TIMES* CROSSWORD PUZ-zle offered the following clue for a five-letter word: "Son of Henry and father of Henry II." I passed by the clue until I had a letter entered from another clue. The word began with "E." Well, that made no sense. King Henry of England surely had a son with a common English name, and I could think of none that began with E and was five letters long.

Aha, I thought, I've been fooled. It's not English mon-archs we are talking about here, but French or Portuguese (think Prince Henry the Navigator) monarchs. I am not an expert on common names or monarchical names in either na-tion, so I waited until I had another letter. The word ended with "L." Huh? What kind of name is this? I hadn't a clue.

Actually, I did have a clue. But I was reading it wrong.

One more letter added: ED_ _L.

Now I knew, but only because I grew up in the 1950s and recalled that the Ford Motor Company's disastrous car, the Edsel, was named after a member of the Ford family, Edsel Ford—the son of Henry Ford and the father of Henry Ford II.

Faced with a problem on which I had an incomplete set of facts (as we almost always are), I asked the wrong question. Because I asked the wrong question, I could not come up with the right answer. Innovators have to do better than that. They are doing their job right when they ask the right question first.

But that's hindsight, you say. "You knew it was the wrong question once you had the right answer. I want to ask the right question first and not waste my time and my company's resources chasing after the answer to the wrong question." Fair enough. And there is a method that will help you achieve that goal, but let us be sure that we understand the concept first.

All of us start from the comfortable. I am familiar with English history, so when I was faced with a question about two persons named Henry and Henry II, I went to where I was comfortable: England.[1] That's a natural reaction, and very often it will lead us to a right result. But not always.

Getting to the Right Question

To get to the right question more certainly, we have to get outside our own skins and take a detached view of the question. That is actually very hard to do. Here's why.

When faced with a question like the crossword clue, people tend to break down into three different types.

People of the first type take the question literally, go into their comfort area, and come up with a single possible answer (e.g., it must be the father of King Henry II of England). Once they reach that answer, all other options are precluded. This type of person, upon learning that Henry II was actually the son of Geoffrey of Anjou, assumes that the crossword editor has made a mistake and puts down the puzzle in self-righteous annoyance. She may even write a letter to the editor.

People of the second type acknowledge at some level that there may be several ways of approaching the problem, but believe that the odds heavily favor the one that they (coincidentally) are most comfortable with. However, upon being faced with an impossible answer (Geoffrey does not fit in five spaces on the puzzle and does not begin with E), these people will realize that there is a trick involved and will start methodically pursuing the other options in the order that is most comfortable. Eventually they will sort out the result.

People of the third type make no assumptions at all about the question. These people look at the question and say, "Henry? Which Henry? Hmmm. They are trying to pull a fast one on me here. They are trying to make me jump to a conclusion that it is the comfortable Henry. I won't do that. What are the other options?"

The first group of people will never innovate. They never ask the right question except by blind luck. We will call them Linear People. They move methodically from step to step, but they are unconcerned about the possibility that their reasoning path started with a false assumption and are unlikely to reexamine that assumption. Such people are often very good at math.

People in the second group may innovate, but they will get there later than the competition. Let us label them Eventual Innovators. This is not a put-down. These people are the heart and soul of any innovation activity because there are so few people in the third category. Eventual Innovators start with assumptions but, when faced with empirical weaknesses in those assumptions, will start over. Many scientists fall into this group.

People in the third group, whom I will call Unassuming Persons, can innovate constantly. They really have no strong assumptions. That makes them curious about everything, and they have a sense of endless wonder. There are not many Unassuming Persons out there because very few people are actually able to be that detached from the assumptions that help us all get through life. It is not surprising to discover that these people often have backgrounds in the arts.

So most innovators will fall into the second category. These people need to develop a regular habit of challenging the conventional wisdom. This takes energy and courage, but it takes a process as well.

This book gives three "right" questions, and the Eventual Innovators should put these questions on a wall in their office because they must constantly remind themselves of the need to get back to basics and confront these questions, just as was necessary in the crossword problem. Getting into the habit of asking these "right" questions will save time and effort and dollars. But that is not the end of the story.

Asking the right question is not enough. It is necessary, but not sufficient. To get things right, we have to have the right answers.

Finding the Right Answers

Let us take the question from Step 1: *What tasks is the product really used for?* It is entirely possible to answer that question incorrectly. Someone could still look at a faucet and answer it by saying, "Customers use this to get water." We know from Chapter 2 that they actually use kitchen faucets to:

- Wash hands.
- Wash dishes.
- Wash food.
- Obtain specific amounts of water for cooking.

But getting to those options required some work on our part. We had to look at a kitchen faucet and try to make the distinction between functions and tasks. We had to step back from our own biases and assumptions and look at something we had seen a million times in a brand new light. We might have done that work well, or we might have done it poorly. How can we know we have gotten to the right answer?

Actually, there are two ways we can know: obviousness and observation. Let us take a look at each.

Obviousness

If you want to innovate, obvious answers to the questions asked in this book are *never* true. Let me repeat that. If you want to innovate, obvious answers to the questions asked in this book are *never* true. Not once. Under no circumstances. Here's why.

The obvious answer will always reflect the existing paradigm. If it is obvious, it is obvious because it fits neatly into the way we view the world. It may extend the product in some way. It may make water flow faster or make it shut off automatically after a certain period of time. Those changes would be positive and would add slightly to the product's value, but again, these are more mutations than innovations. You, as an innovator, want to move beyond these types of changes into a complete rethinking of the product so that it serves its tasks with maximum efficiency, not just with marginal improvement. Why describe your product as "better" when you can describe it as "best"?

Let us look at an example. Assume that the year is 1960 or so and you are running the Subway Token Department for the New York City Transit Authority. You are conscientious about your work, and you decide to ask customers for their opinions on your subway tokens. Well, it turns out that they do not like your dime-sized tokens. It is worse than that: They hate your tokens. Your tokens are so small that they get lost in pockets and purses. You have to keep them separate from your coins or else you will be sorting through dimes and pennies to pull out a token. They slip from your hand when you are getting ready to put them in the slot. You have to wait in line to buy them. There is really nothing good to be said about these tokens.

What can you do? The quick fix (and the one that was actually used starting in 1970) is to change the size of the token. Make it big enough to stick out in a pocket full of change and easier to grasp at the same time. This is the obvious solution, and it suffers from all the characteristics of obvious solutions. It is not an innovation; it is merely a design change along the path of the existing paradigm. Customers will be somewhat happier because the change will reduce some of their problems. But unless you give a token a two-inch diameter, the larger tokens will still be somewhat difficult to distinguish, and you will still have to wait in line to buy them. They make the task of entering the subway somewhat more efficient, but there is still a lot of room for improvement.

The innovative answer is to say that the problem is with tokens themselves. They are inherently like coins, and so they will always be confusing. They are good for only one trip, and so you will frequently need to buy more. Moreover, they limit your pricing structure to "one token fits all."

When we look at the task involved and reject the obvious solution, we are forced to ask ourselves, "How would I do this in a world without tokens? How can I avoid coinlike objects, allow multiple trips with the same entry device, and, ideally, give myself more pricing flexibility?" The innovative answer (implemented in 1976 in the Washington, D.C., Metro and, finally, in 2003 in New York) is a debit card. It is easy to buy and provides for many trips. It is not going to be confused with a coin, and it allows an infinite variety of pricing options. Users save time and effort. The subway system does so as well: It employs fewer people since it does not have to sell and collect tokens anymore.[2]

But this answer, this innovation, did not take place and could not take place until the paradigm was shifted, until the underlying assumption was abandoned. With subway tokens, the underlying assumption was that the problem was in the design of the tokens. In fact, the problem was with the use of tokens as a means of gaining entry to the subway. The user wanted to complete the task of getting on a train, but the product owners were focused on something entirely different—optimizing the design of subway tokens.

So the obvious is not the innovative. But it should not be totally discarded. As we will see later on in Chapter 10, "The Human Factor," you can draw a distinction between **BIG** innovations and small innovations. If enough small innovations are added to a product, they may make a significant change in the value proposition, so these innovations are not to be ignored. But we get further, faster with touchdowns than with field goals, so when you see an obvious improvement, do not settle for it. The obvious should be the fallback position, not the starting position.

Observation

So much of innovation has to do with observation. If we see someone filling a pot with water from a kitchen faucet and our observation is, "Faucets supply water," we have no place to go. But if we stop and say, "What is really going on here?

What is this person trying to accomplish? How can I help him accomplish that?" then we have a genuine chance of breaking through to new ground.

Just as observation is a key element of innovative ideas, so too is it the best testing ground for those ideas because reality is the best testing ground for almost anything. Does your answer to the question fit with what people actually do? Can you observe the behavior of people using your product and see if your answer is correct? Does your innovation solve old problems, but create new ones?

Let us go back to our kitchen faucet. One of the proposed innovations was premeasured water. Push a button once for one cup, twice for two cups, and so on. That sounds right, but its correctness depends on whether people actually do things the way they are supposed to do them.

The recipe calls for three cups of water. Does the cook actually measure three cups, or does she simply put *roughly* three cups of water into the pot? If the measurement for one recipe is rough, is that true of all or most recipes?

I make bread by hand. I make rough measurements of my flour and water because as I knead the bread by hand, I know from a touch trained through making hundreds of loaves of bread whether more water or more flour is needed. In that case, rough measurements are fine. If, on the other hand, I made bread by machine, I would measure quite precisely because the ratio is important and I would have no chance to adjust it once the machine starts kneading.

So if one is making bread by machine or cooking rice (which does require precise measurement), the exact amount of water may matter. But if one is making pasta, a little extra water probably will not hurt anything. And if a little extra water won't hurt anything, the value of our innovation is low.

If we observe enough cooks preparing enough recipes, we will begin to get a sense of whether our proposed innovation makes sense. Does it add value because it would be used all the time by a good percentage of the potential users? Or is it just a "feature" that may help to sell the product but won't actually be used (or valued) much in the end?

This latter situation arises quite often. An innovation is made that is undeniably superior to the old way of doing things. But the old behavior is deeply ingrained and well understood, so the motivation to change one's behavior has to be very high for change to actually take place.

Some years ago, a software product that I was managing moved from green dots on a black screen to a graphical user interface (GUI). Over the next few years, all new development was done in the GUI, but some customers still stuck to the earlier version. Eventually the day came when we had to pull the plug on that old product. It would strain your credulity if I described the outpouring of anger and anguish we received over that decision—even though we were offering the users something that was enormously superior at absolutely no cost to them. People who have gotten used to doing things a certain way are often uninterested in investing in change, and a change that may seem easy for the innovator may in fact be quite difficult for the user who is a linear thinker.

Observation will tell you whether you have a problem here or not. And observation does not have to be expensive.

Prototyping can usually be done inexpensively. Even describing an innovation or using good drawings can evoke a reaction from users. That reaction may tell you whether it is wise to invest more funds in the innovation or not. If you do invest more and can create a working model or prototype, then you can engage in more objective observations. The users will tell you whether they like the innovation or not and whether they would actually use it or not. That observed information is a lot more valuable than what comes out of most focus groups or surveys. It allows the product developer to see at once what is good and what is bad about an idea. It can be the springboard for many other ideas as well.

Of course, what is being described here is the scientific method. You develop a thesis. Then you create an experiment to test the thesis. You observe the results of the experiment and compare them to the thesis. You publish the details of your experiment and its results. Then you gather criticism of your experiment from others. Finally, you see whether the experiment can be duplicated by others with the same result.

The great virtue of the scientific method is its objectivity. If the experiment proves the thesis to be false, the scientist moves on. Would that this were so in the world of product innovation!

If you have done product development work for any period of time, you will have seen developers who were so taken by their own idea that they:

1. Did not test at all.
2. Tested in such a way as to ensure that the results matched the thesis.

3. Ignored the negative results and latched on firmly to some isolated positive statements.
4. Transferred learnings from another market to a new one without validating them in the new one.
5. Did all of the above and created a great press release as well.

Such shenanigans are entirely understandable. They are usually defended by statements like, "I have been in this market for 10 years, and I know this market" or some other form of self-validation.

But they can lead to ridiculous results. I have a colleague who is legally blind. He performs a highly technical job through the use of special equipment. For instance, he has a computer screen that enlarges letters many times. He recently informed me that there was a new cell phone available for people in his situation. It had large keys and a larger screen, and it magnified the characters on the screen.

This was great. Some product developer somewhere had recognized that there was a market that was not being served and moved in to serve it. Just one thing: It came equipped with a camera. Even the briefest of test periods would have shown that there are not a lot of blind photographers, so the camera was superfluous, and leaving it out would have saved the manufacturer and the buyer a few bucks.

This is a serious problem, and it is a cultural problem. Cultural problems are particularly intractable, but these problems must be confronted. It is very rare that the financial decision to create a new product is based on deep knowledge of the market research. It is more often based on a summary prepared by the product advocate. The fox not only guards the henhouse, but is the only source that management has for what is going on in it.

Checking Your Answer

There is no reason for this reliance on the fox. As we will discuss in Chapter 12, there are several methods that a business can use to determine whether the innovator's thesis has been objectively tested. These include:

1. *Publication.* The innovation should be summarized and distributed to a wide range of people throughout the organization for comment. This will help weed out bad ideas at an early stage, and it will lead to improvements in good ideas as well.

2. *Peer review.* Every organization should have a Chief Cynical Officer whose job it is to poke holes in product proposals. That person will probably have trouble finding people to have lunch with, but a position like this would save every organization a lot of money. In many organizations, finance people take on this role. But they are generally the least knowledgeable about the product and have spent the least time with customers. Their knowledge base limits their ability to be really effective cynics. They are cynical about numbers, but they have no credibility or expertise in being cynical about products.

3. *Replications by an outside group.* Before investing $10 million in a new product, get an outside research group to conduct its own experiment.

4. *Pilot testing (where that makes economic sense).* Pilots are a fabulous way of testing a thesis. However, they can often cost a substantial portion of the whole development budget, so they do not always make sense. But pilots can also be simple. In the late 1960s, I was a student at Notre Dame. The Hesburgh Library (where the famed Touchdown Jesus can be seen hovering over the football stadium during telecasts) had just been completed, and it was in a part of campus that was just being built on. One day, as the library was being opened for business, I noticed something startling: There were no paths to the building. It was all a sea of grass. As time went by, students walked to the library, and earthen paths gradually began to emerge. Come spring, the concrete trucks moved in and put down permanent paths where the students had "marked" them. No one would ever have drawn the paths the way the students actually ended up making them, but this simple pilot ensured that the "product" was perfectly suited to the users' needs, and doing it cost nothing.

Again, these notions mimic the scientific method. But there is nothing wrong with that. It is simple. It is clear. And it works. There is always great pressure to come up with new products and then move them to market rapidly. The sales force needs to be fed. The competition needs to be bested.

And that "stretch" number made up out of thin air by head-quarters needs to be met. But even in the relatively short run, the economics favor observation to make sure you have it right. *Relaunch* is the ugliest word in the product developer's vocabulary. Relaunches eat up resources needed for the next year's products. They eat up marketing dollars convincing customers that "this time" you have it right. And they cost you credibility in the marketplace. There is no pitch harder than the one that begins, "That product we sold you six months ago turns out to be a loser, so we have a new and improved version for you."

"A stitch in time saves nine" is still a pretty good motto to have on your wall.

Chapter 4

Mutation or Innovation?

I GREW UP IN NEW JERSEY (EXIT 159). COMPARED TO MY CUR-
rent domicile in Minnesota, things were edgier. Speech was
more direct. Confrontation was a part of life and was cher-
ished. Truth came without hesitation and without makeup
on. And the expressions were a bit more colorful.

Cars were a big part of our lives and were a significant
determinant of status. Much time was spent discussing them,
and we boys all thought ourselves experts on the subject. One
day, on the bus on the way to school, someone was describing
the car he had just purchased and was working on. I do not
recall the make or model, but it was not a type of car that
would inspire envy among his peers.

He described in detail the things he had done to sport up
the car: leather-covered steering wheel, a new floor-mounted

gear shifter, a gleaming chrome cover for the air filter. When he got to this last item, a voice from a couple of rows back uttered the words: "If it don't go—chrome it!" There was nothing more to say. This piece of wisdom had summarized it all. His car was no different from what it had been before. It just looked a little different, and that look did not mask or overcome its underlying inadequacies. "Putting lipstick on a pig" is a more bucolic variation of the same notion.

Just as activity does not equal progress, so change does not equal innovation. Once it has been stated, this is obvious, but it is amazing how often the concept is ignored.

For instance, Toyota is a company that is justly proud of its product. Utterly dependable, reasonably inexpensive, comfortable, and safe to drive, Toyota is the cream of the basic vehicle. I drive one myself, and while the friends of my youth might not regard it as prestigious, I like it very much, largely because it is absolutely reliable and will be for many years. Underneath all of this plain vanilla good stuff, Toyota is also a leading innovator in technology and design. Having established a brand that stands for reliability, Toyota seems to be interested in gaining more recognition for its innovative side. And while it clearly has a lot to brag about there, I was a little taken aback by a two-page Toyota ad spread in *Newsweek* in May 2006.

The ad began by pointing out that all cars now have good safety systems in them. It then asked a rather startling question about your safety when you are *not* in an accident. Well, I hadn't thought about that subject, I will admit, but that tells you something in and of itself. If I had not previously been worried about my safety while I was in an auto and not in an accident, what was Toyota trying to tell me? Had I missed something?

Apparently I had, and the something I had missed was germs.

Toyota was introducing the Plasmacluster ionizer. This device would send out positive and negative ions that would wrap themselves around germs and render them harmless to you.

In addition, in the same ad, Toyota announced that its seats were now covered with Fraichir, a treatment that would prevent your skin from getting dry.

Now, America is a big country, chock full of people with different tastes and interests, but in my heart of hearts, I do not think that there are many folks other than Michael Jackson who spend a lot of time worrying about germs in their car. I have an air filter and an ionization system at home, and so, I suppose, I would be the target audience for this feature, since this would seem to indicate an above-average interest in combating germs. But I just stared in disbelief when I saw the ad. While Michael might find this feature attractive, I think it is unlikely that there are many people who would be willing to spend money to combat germs in their car.

And as to the seat fabrics that treat your dry skin, this might be useful at nudist camps, but it is hard to see that this changes the product experience for most people.

The ad copy refers to these features as innovations. Well, maybe they are in the sense that no one had ever thought to put them in a car before (with good reason, in my view). But to me, these are mere mutations—chrome air filter covers moved forward 40 years. They make some change in the product, but not the kind of change that makes a difference.

How Do You Know It's a Mutant?

But how can we tell the difference between mutations and innovations? In the end, we cannot. We do not buy the product, we build it. It is users who will tell us whether something is an innovation or a mutation. Do not get me wrong. Users will buy mutations. There is something to be said aesthetically for chrome air filter covers, and there is a market for aesthetic improvements in cars. But chrome is the innovation; chrome air filter covers are just an application of that innovation.

Users will tell us whether or not something is a true innovation by their reactions to the change. Real innovation is clear to the user at once. It will not have been obvious before but, once revealed, it immediately evokes a reaction from the user, and that reaction is focused on *utility*, not on *appearance* or *novelty*.

This trio is significant. Each one represents a form of change, and each one can appear to be innovative, but only a useful change is really innovation.

There is a kind of Darwinian logic to this. Natural selection favors useful variations in the species. A fluorescent species of bird might be beautiful, but it is not useful. Indeed, fluorescence would aid predators at night and thus would be a negative change in utility. On the other hand, a beak shape that is better able to extract seeds would be a useful change.

Similarly, nature tolerates, but does not reward, novelty without utility in single organisms. Having different-colored eyes is novel, but it is not useful. It does not aid an animal in hunting food, defending against predators, or reproducing. So, while nature may not eliminate the trait, it does not encourage it either.

Nature tends to tolerate many changes in appearance, to punish true novelty (as in certain types of genetic mutations that are rarely passed on), and to reward real innovation. So, too, with the market. It rewards real innovation and quickly kills off mere novelty as fad. Appearance carries some weight, but not as much as utility. You can produce a purple faucet, but doing so will not change the game unless there is some utility added as well.

Since the distinction between these three types of change is so important, let us spend a few minutes going through each.

Appearance

Changes in appearance are probably the most common form of product variation.

You will remember that in the faucet scenario, this was really what the industry was doing, and it is probably what most readers focused on as well. There is a certain logic to this. People are attracted to pretty things. If we view our job as marketing, rather than innovation, then "pretty" will do for a while. If we can grab some market share through style changes, then we have gained share at a rather low price. But what we can do cheaply, so can the other guy, and the battle of the pretty faucets has no winner in the end. By the time the designers are through, each player will have developed a line of faucets for every taste, and market share will be right back where it was.

In short, pretty does not last. When product development is down to esthetics, it is on its last legs. It is time to restaff the organization because the people doing the job have run out of ideas that make a difference. There is nothing wrong with pretty. Products should be esthetically pleasing. Look at Apple. It has created innovation after innovation, and then topped itself in product design as well. The combination is mutually supportive. A significant product innovation packaged in a stunning design is very hard to beat.

Indeed, one way to announce an innovation is through design. If people see a unique design, they are prepared to accept the idea that it is part of an innovative product. But design by itself is treadmill innovation. It is a lot of activity that, when you are done, leaves you in precisely the same spot you started at.

Novelty

Novelty is a far more subtle trap. Novelty has a certain "wow" factor to it. Right now, in a Toyota showroom somewhere, a prospective car buyer is being told about the germ-proof car environment and is saying, "Wow. You guys think of everything." Actually, she is probably also thinking about the bragging rights available when she drives the car to work.

"Does that Audi of yours have germ protection?"

But will our driver actually ever notice the difference? Probably not. It is unlikely that she will be keeping track of all of her colds over a ten-year period and comparing it with the prior ten years. It is unlikely that, when the driver does not get avian flu, she will say, "Getting that ionizer was sure a smart move." It is very unlikely that the next time she goes to buy a car, the conversation with the dealer will begin, "Don't show me anything unless it has an ionizer in it."

We can distinguish mere novelties from real innovations fairly easily. The really simple test is to show the change to someone and wait to see if he describes it as "cool." That pretty much settles the matter. Cool is often clever, but it is rarely useful. We are attracted to cool and we will tell our friends about it, but not many of us will buy it.

There is one group that will buy cool: the infamous early adopters. You know them. They have a closet full of gadgets that are undeniably cool, but their lack of usefulness is demonstrated by their place alongside the eight-track tape player and the Newton pocket computer in that closet.

A small group of people may buy cool, but most people buy useful, and no one buys the same cool more than once. Novelty, like appearance, is a short-term play unless the novelty has deep underlying values that add utility to the product.

The word *novelty* itself derives from the Latin *novellus,* meaning "new" or "not previously seen." This leads to another way to determine if something is merely a novelty. Do the marketing folks want to call it "New Widget" or "New Whatchamacallit"? If they do, it is because they cannot figure out any attribute of it that is substantively different from what you used to sell. They cannot see the utility in the change.

If they don't see an actual benefit, neither will your customers.

Utility

The things that we buy can all be classified as either useful or beautiful. We seek to gain either some practical advantage or some aesthetic gratification when we spend our money. And, ideally, we get both. We buy curtains to maintain privacy, but we focus on their color and style. We buy furniture to sit in, but we test it for comfort before we buy it. But among the equally comfortable, we choose the most attractive. We buy a blue car because we like the color blue, but we buy a brand of blue car that we regard as safe, mechanically sound, and filled with the features that we believe are valuable. We may be interested in looks when we buy, but we do not buy on looks alone. Utility is the reason we went shopping in the first place.

A closer look at cars may be valuable because cars are typically the second most expensive item we purchase, and because people typically expend real effort in selecting and buying a car.

We buy cars to get from place to place. Our purchase decision is typically very practical. A survey conducted by J.D. Power and Associates for the *Detroit News* found that the top four reasons (out of 21) that American car buyers rejected American cars were:[1]

1. Reliability and durability
2. Quality of workmanship
3. Resale value
4. Fuel economy

The vehicle's style came in seventh and vehicle image came in ninth. Nineteen of the 21 factors listed were practical—safety, pricing, availability of parts, and so forth.

These are highly utilitarian factors. While we might find a different slant among Ferrari buyers and an even stronger utilitarian slant among lower-end buyers, for most of us these figures sound about right.

We select the brand and model first. Both of these options tilt toward utilitarian factors because brands and models are surrogates for certain specific traits in the highly segmented automobile market. These days we may select model and brand based on a review in *Consumer Reports* or through research conducted on the Internet. *Consumer Reports* may mention the beauty of a car it is reviewing, but it is much more interested in the ease with which child safety seats can be installed, the repair history, and the gas mileage. Independent Internet sites provide real users' comments on the vehicles. Those comments are overwhelmingly focused on practical matters—mileage, handling, frequency of repair, helpfulness of dealers, and so on. The complaints are practical as well. They might say:

"Parts are hard to get."
"The trim pieces have a tendency to come off."
"Cup holders will not take a large cup from a fast-food chain."

All of this utilitarian information leads us to select a brand and model consistent with our own needs.

Once we have selected a make and model, we select a dealer that carries the car we are interested in. If we have a choice, we will probably ask around among friends and co-workers, looking for their experience. We will want to know the dealer's reputation for good prices, fair dealing, low-hassle negotiations, standing by its products, quality of repairs, and the like.

At the dealer's, we will select a specific car based on color and features. Some people will give more weight to color than to a navigation system. Others will take any color as long as the car has such a system. So, whereas looks begin to play a role at the narrow end of the buying funnel, the great bulk of the decision making is focused on the utilitarian aspects of the product. We assume that the color and the other style features that we want will be available.

Just How Innovative Is This Concept?

What does all of this really mean? It means that every proposed product innovation can be analyzed along these three axes. For the typical buyer, utility will be of the highest value, followed (distantly in most cases) by appearance. Novelty will lag way behind. This provides an interesting, inexpensive, and fast way to filter proposed innovations at a very early stage. Consider the following approach:

Please rate this product for each statement on a scale of 1 to 5, with 5 meaning that you strongly support the statement and 1 meaning that you do not support the statement.

	1	2	3	4	5
This product would, in balance, improve my life.					
This product would look good in my house.					
This product is unlike anything I have seen before.					

Anything that gets three 5s is a home run. But anything that gets a 1 in Utility (the first row) is a loser no matter how high it scores in the other categories. The venerable Lava Lamp provides a good example. Assume the year is 1959 and the first Lava Lamps are coming on the market. You are in the lamp department at a now-defunct department store looking for a bedside lamp. You see the Lava Lamp, and you certainly give it a 5 in the "This product is unlike anything I have seen before" category. You may even give it a 5 in the "This product would look good in my house" category, depending on your taste. But if you want the lamp to read by, you probably will rank it very low in the "This product would, in balance, improve my life" line. And so you will not buy it for this purpose. You might, instead, buy one as decoration for your living room, but you would buy another lamp for bedtime reading.

Of course, there are many more sophisticated (and expensive) forms of market research. But this approach is simple, can be conducted with only a description or drawing of a product, and gets to the heart of things. It allows you to test the product concept without any significant expense or delay.

A deep-dive research activity in a focus group or the like can tell you a lot about what details matter in a product and how that product should be positioned, but it is a poor mechanism for validating the concept itself. Why? Let me give you an example.

I once had a product idea that I thought was sensational. It was an industry changer, I thought. We presented it to two focus groups through a PowerPoint show that went through a fair amount of the details. The facilitator worked off a carefully prepared script and was very experienced and thoroughly prepared.

The first focus group went off like a dream. This was way better than sliced bread. When could they buy this? Could they tell their friends about it? When asked to give it a numerical rating, they gave it 9 out of 10, the highest rating of any product we had ever presented.

The second focus group took place immediately after the first, using the same segmentation, the same facilitator, and the same script and presentation. When the presentation was completed, the first person to speak focused on a feature that he did not like. This feature was not essential to the product, but the whole group got on the bandwagon and would talk of nothing else. This group ended up giving the product a 3. But, when the facilitator asked the group members to state how much productivity gain they would get out of the product, the lowest answer was 10 percent.

Now, truthfully, it is not possible for a product to be a 3 out of 10 and simultaneously give you at least a 10 percent boost in productivity. But the focus group is really an unfocused instrument. We ask for so much information from it in such a short space of time that there is a great risk, as here, that the forest will get lost in the trees. And it is the forest we care about.

The information from the second focus group was useful in positioning the product for the market, but it was pretty much useless in evaluating the product. Even the first focus group was of very little real value in the end. Sure, it feels great to hear 10 people praise your product concept, but these people never spotted the issue that dominated the second group, and so, as a practical matter, they were not much help.

If the concept is right, if the product innovation offers actual utility, then the kind of details a focus group can enlighten you on can be taken care of later. Of course you want to get it as right as you can as early as you can, but if you offer your customers a 10 percent gain in productivity, very few of them will say, "No thanks. I think I'll wait until you figure out those last couple of wrinkles."

Net Utility

What is important in testing for utility is that you test for net utility. It is one thing to say to a customer: "Would you find it useful to have a voice-operated word processor?" The answer is a universal, "Yes!" But what happens if the question is changed to: "Would you find it useful to have a voice-operated word processor? It will require you to spend two hours reading various sentences into it so that it can 'tune' to your voice and pronunciation, and it will get one out of one hundred words wrong at the end, so you will have to reread and edit your manuscript with some care."

In that situation (which somewhat exaggerates the state of these dictation programs), the odds are pretty good that customers will not be lining up outside your door. For such a product to succeed, it must show a net utility that clearly demonstrates a higher level of productivity than manual typing. For dictation software, that may be true for certain classes of customers. Such programs are no doubt a boon to the physically handicapped, for instance. There are some people who compose better by speaking than they do by typing. These niches will be served well even by a balky program. But to cross over into the general market, the average user will need to decide that the dictation software has a positive net utility.

There is a simple preliminary way to test for net utility, and that is to apply the use case. A use case is a description of the product idea in the context in which it would be used. It is a means of taking the product idea out of the abstract world in which it is designed and into the concrete world where it will be used. For example, you have an idea that people would use a device that would allow a book to be read from a portable electronic device—you think of it as an e-book. It is a very exciting idea when you look at the end of the process—the smiling user sitting on an airplane with a paper-thin electronic device from which she is reading *War and Peace*. But the concept takes on a different dimension when you walk through the mechanics of subscribing to a service for book downloads, working through copy-protection schemes, wondering about battery life, and the like. This walkthrough of the use case is very useful in product design because as we walk through the use of a product in detail, we begin to see what features are excess and what additional features might be added. We see where the weaknesses are instead of just the strengths. And even for the strengths, we get a much clearer idea of what those strengths mean in practical terms to real-life users. That information will be invaluable a little further down the road.

It is possible to envision successful product development without market research, but it is not possible to envision successful product development without careful application of the use case. It is the first moment in the product development cycle when you put yourself in the customer's shoes. It is when you find your customer's pleasures and feel her pain, and that moment is the moment of truth.

The use case is simple to apply and costs nothing. Find the three most cynical people you know (or requisition some from the Chief Cynical Officer) and describe to them how the product would be used in the real world. Talk through it in as much detail as you can. Let them know something about the different types of users. A student may use an e-book quite differently from an executive. Notice whether you start feeling that you are trying to convince yourself. Let your audience ask questions, and be prepared to give honest answers.

Videotape the exercise if possible. A day or two later, review the tape. Watch yourself as you describe the use case, and pay close attention to the reactions you get. Is your audience being polite but is not convinced? Do you look like someone who believes in the product idea, or someone who is simply trying to sell it? Would you buy the product after hearing your own description? If you are honest with yourself and you view the responses objectively, you will know very quickly whether you have come up with an innovation or only a novelty or better-looking widget.

It is time to turn to Step 2. It may be useful at this time for you to refresh yourself on Step 1 (What tasks is the product really used for?) and to contemplate a bit the important matter of net utility. The focus on task and the importance of the user's having a strong sense of having gained time, money, or productivity will matter a good deal in the Chapter 5, where these ideas will be directly applied and expanded on.

Step 2: Making Life Simpler

In CHAPTER 2, WE DISCUSSED THE PROBLEM OF DISTINGUISHing between a function and a task. We saw that the function is what a product does and the task is what a user does *with* the product. All true product innovation takes place at the task level because innovation is in the eye of the user, not of the engineering department. Improvement in function is not a bad thing, of course. A faucet that lasts longer or needs less maintenance is a good thing. But this is not really innovation from the user's perspective. Users expect good functioning in the products they buy. They expect that they will finish their task using the product. But they want to finish their task efficiently. And since users are the ones who buy the product, their focus on the task needs to be our focus as well.

This analysis led us to:

Step 1: What tasks is the product really used for?

That question is enormously useful. You must answer that question with care and insight in order to innovate. But once you have answered it, you are not necessarily through. Let us look at an everyday object that has been innovated (and mutated) to death: the automobile. Most families have one. Lots of families have two or even more. But when we ask ourselves, "What tasks is the product used for?" we find that there are really several.

A car may be primarily used for commuting back and forth to work. It may be used to cart children to and from school and activities. It may be used typically for shopping and other errands. Each use case suggests a different set of tasks, and each different set of tasks has product innovation connotations. How is the poor product developer supposed to work his way through this thicket and into the sweet spot of product innovation?

Which task are we supposed to focus on, and, more importantly, what do we do when we figure that out?

The answer to the first part of the question is easy: You focus on all the tasks. That is what customers deserve for their money. If any substantial number of customers is using that car to bring ice to the desert, then you need to make sure that the vehicle performs that task as well as it can, so in theory you put a good freezer compartment in it. If customers are using their car to haul a high school basketball team to a gymnasium, then that is the task that you need to think about, and you might, in theory, want to make the roof a little higher and put a little extra legroom in as well.

Unfortunately, practical matters interfere with theory,

and we cannot build a custom car for every buyer. What we can do is identify the tasks that typical customers do with their car.

But, having identified these tasks, what's next?

This is where Step 2 comes in.

Some Really Smart Ideas

Rather than just reveal the question, let us look at some product innovations (real and imaginary) and see what lessons we can draw from them. We will start in my grandmother's kitchen in Jersey City sometime in the 1950s.

My grandmother's kitchen was distinguished by four things. First, there were the geraniums that seemed to permanently bloom on the windowsill. Second, there was the large, round washing machine that was in the middle of the kitchen, looking like a barrel on four legs with an attached wringer, which, along with the clothesline on pulleys outside the kitchen window, constituted the dryer. Third, there was my grandmother herself, small enough to fit easily into that washing machine and skinny enough to have a shot at making it through the wringer. Finally, there was the toaster.

The toaster was bright chrome and was shaped like a wedge of pie standing on its wide end. On each side was a flap that you could pull down in order to place a piece of bread inside the toaster. You then closed the flaps, turned on the toaster, and pulled down the flaps again after a minute or so. When you did that, the bread came down with it, and you could see if the side facing up was adequately toasted. If it was, you turned it over and repeated the operation for the other side. The center held the heating wires, which glowed red and whose heat was reflected to the other side of the toast to some degree by the chrome panel. I thought it was quite wonderful, and I regretted that at our house, the whole toasting process was hidden away in the pop-up mechanism. It seemed to me then like a very inferior way to make toast.

But eventually, progress made it to my grandmother's walk-up in Jersey City, and she had her own pop-up toaster. I suspect it was a gift.

Fast forward to the 1960s. I had received my driver's license, and I quickly learned one of the most important lessons that any driver in New Jersey needed to know: Carry plenty of quarters. A few miles drive down the Garden State Parkway at the northern end of that infamous road could bring you to five tollbooths. The lines at the change booths were long, so you wanted to have the exact change you needed for the self-serve baskets. Besides, it was more fun to try to go through the booth as fast as you could while throwing the quarter into the basket and hoping that the wooden barrier would come up in time.

Even more challenging was the New Jersey Turnpike. There you received a toll card when you entered that had to be presented when you exited, and your toll was based on the number of exits you had traveled. This had to be calculated and money presented and change counted before you were on your way again. This took a long time, and long lines were very common at important exits.

Today, cars drive right through the tollbooths on the

turnpike without stopping if they have EZ-Pass, a device that acts like a debit card; it is placed on your windshield and detected and read by the computer at the tollbooth. No change needed. No waiting in lines. No wasted gas.

Now let's move back in time again to 1928. A native of Davenport, Iowa, named Otto F. Rohwedder traveled to Chillicothe, Missouri, to deliver the first version of his new invention, the bread slicer. The enlightened purchaser saw his business grow twenty-fold in just two weeks. This invention was the last great innovation *not* referred to as the "greatest thing since sliced bread." Rohwedder accomplished the extraordinary feat of taking a product—bread—that had been a commodity for 7,000 years and innovating with it. His feat is celebrated in Chillicothe on Sliced Bread Day (July 7). And so it should be. Few inventions have had as much daily impact.

Now we will travel to Thalwil, Switzerland. It is 2002, and I am newly ensconced in an office with a view of Lake Zurich and the Alps. Well, most of the time I have that view. Somewhere in the building, there is a computer that is calculating how much sunlight is pouring into my office. As soon as that computer decides that it is probably too bright for me to do my work or that it will get too hot in the office (since the Swiss view air-conditioning as unhealthy), it issues a command, and aluminum louvers roll down and then close. Those of you who are familiar with the sci-fi classic *Forbidden Planet* will know what that is like.

Perhaps you are getting the idea, but let me throw in a couple more examples to round out the point.

It used to be that Tide detergent was Tide detergent. If

you wanted bleach, you bought it from Clorox and added that separately at a specified time in the cycle. Then the washing machine was adjusted so that you could add the detergent to one repository and the bleach to another, and the machine would release each at the appropriate time. Then Tide added bleach to its product so that you did not have to add the bleach yourself.

But as time passed, having clean and bright clothes was not enough. They had to be soft as well. So you were back to the practice of adding fabric softener at the appropriate time. Soon the washing machine did that for you, and then—guess what?—Tide now comes with a Touch of Downy fabric softener.

Propane-powered barbecue grills are everywhere. But places to refill the propane tanks are pretty hard to find. When you do find one, you have to get the attendant to go out to the tank, unlock it, refill your tank, charge you, and send you on your way. But companies like Quick Tank allow you to drive up to any convenience store, drop off your tank, and pick up a full one.

Just one more item, and then on to Step 2.

My notes for this chapter included a product I called "self-inflating tires." I had an image of a set of tires with valves pointing inward and attached to hoses that were, in turn, attached to a compressed air cylinder. The cylinder would be kept filled by a pump driven by the engine. This was a great idea! Your tires would always be inflated to the proper pressure. The tires would last longer, and you would get better gas mileage. Safety would be enhanced as well because the pump system would detect if a tire was steadily losing air and alert you to the problem. I cannot tell you how clever I felt. I was starting to think up brand names and whom I would line up as investors when I decided, out of an abundance of caution, to check the Internet.

You guessed it. Go to http://www.selfinflatingtire.com to learn more. I still think it's a great idea, and I wish I had thought of it first.

A Focus on Efficiency

All right, you say, that's a nice list of good innovations, but what lesson can be drawn from it? Look back through the list and see if you can determine the commonality. It is not very tricky, but it is very important. Here is the list. Spend a moment or two thinking about it.

1. Pop-up toaster
2. EZ-Pass
3. Automatic window shutters
4. Tide with Downy softener
5. Quick Tank propane tanks
6. Self-inflating tires

You probably know the answer, but just in case, here it is. Each one of these product innovations does exactly the same thing: It removes one or more steps from a task. Pop-up toasters toast both sides of the bread at once and turn off when the toasting is done. EZ-Pass allows us to proceed through the New Jersey Turnpike without accepting a toll card, stopping at a booth to have the toll calculated, handing over cash, and getting change. Automatic window shutters keep the glare out of our eyes and keep our un-air-conditioned offices cooler without our having to do anything. Tide with Downy eliminates the steps of measuring and pouring fabric softener. Quick Tank lets you skip the refilling steps for propane tanks. And self-inflating tires save us the steps of going to the service station, checking our tire pressure with a gauge found in the bottom of the glove compartment, adding air to the tires, checking the pressure again, and repeating the process until the pressure is right.

And the list of examples is nearly endless. Sitting in our kitchen as I write this, I can see a frost-free refrigerator with an ice crusher built in, a self-cleaning oven, a dishwasher, and an espresso maker that is self-bleeding. In fact, I can actually see sliced bread. The phrase, "This is the greatest thing since sliced bread" encapsulates the goal of an innovator: saving actual work in the completion of a task. The saving of work represents utility, and remember, net utility is what innovation is all about.

And that leads us to Step 2:

Step 2: When I know what task a product is really used for, are there any steps that I can remove from that task?

Let us examine this concept. It starts out with an assumption: that every task consists of multiple steps. That probably is not always true, but it is generally true. You have already seen a couple of examples of this. First, there was the list of steps involved in washing your hands. Then there were the steps that we replaced in the Find & Print product. It will be worthwhile spending some time methodically dissecting a task, though, because the difference between steps and tasks is as important as the difference between tasks and functions. When you develop a good, instinctive feel for these differences, you can innovate in any field because it is these two skills that make you an innovator. Among innovators, those with the most creativity and the most customer and product knowledge will be most likely to produce the biggest innovations. But these dissecting skills are the table stakes for all.

The task we will dissect is hanging a picture. This is a mundane task. It is probably an annual occurrence in most households. A new picture is acquired and an old one is moved to a new location, or a room is repainted and all the pictures need rehanging. However often it occurs, it is a pain. The pain comes from three sources: the need to find and gather rarely used equipment (hammer, picture hangers, pencil, and measuring tape), the need to engage in a series of what can be complicated calculations regarding the placement of the picture and then the hanger, and the need to insert the hanger in the correct spot without damaging the wall unduly.

We will start by compiling a list of the steps involved and then see where the opportunities for innovation are.

Creating a list of steps can be very subjective. One person might describe the process "Measure the distance from the ceiling to the height for the picture and mark that spot with a pencil" as one step. Another person might describe the same process as two steps: "Measure the distance from the ceiling to the height for the picture" and "Mark that spot on the wall."

For our purposes, the second approach is correct. *Every*

step has only one verb, every verb means a new step, and every verb has only one object. Verbs are action words, as we learned in grammar school. Action is work. When we eliminate work, we gain utility. Net utility is the goal of innovation. So, innovation exists in the verbs.

Here, then, is the list of steps in picture hanging:

1. Collect pencil.
2. Collect hammer.
3. Collect picture hanger.
4. Collect measuring tape.
5. Determine rough horizontal location.
6. Determine rough vertical location.
7. Measure the distance from the ceiling to the top of the picture.
8. Add to that number the distance between the top of the picture and the center of the stretched picture wire.
9. At your rough horizontal location, measure down from the ceiling to the height indicated by your calculation in Step 8.
10. Place a mark.
11. Measure horizontally from a reference point such as a wall to set your exact horizontal location.
12. Place a mark.
13. With your measuring tape, draw a horizontal line from your horizontal mark across the imagined line of the vertical mark.
14. With your measuring tape, extend a line from your vertical mark across the horizontal line.
15. Nail your picture hanger at this intersection.

16. Erase the remaining pencil lines.
17. Hang the picture.
18. Replace the pencil.
19. Replace the hammer.
20. Replace the measuring tape.

Or, alternatively, you could eyeball the location, pound a nail in, hang the damned picture up, then go back and watch a football game.

What we see, of course is 20 steps to hang one picture. That is an awful lot of work, and there must be millions of people out there who just hate this task. But for you this is a goldmine. You do not see 20 steps. You see 20 opportunities to innovate! You see the chance to make customers happy and to gain wealth yourself!

But first you have to select among these 20 opportunities, and in doing so, you should be mindful of the need for net utility. The highest net utility is the sweet spot here. The sweet spot is that set of steps that best combines the greatest reduction of work for the user with the lowest pain to adopt. If you find that sweet spot and eliminate the steps involved, then you can deal with the other steps as you choose. The user will focus on the greatest net utility gain.

That may need some explanation.

Applying Net Utility

Net utility exists on a continuum. That continuum has two axes: value to the customer and cost to the customer in terms of price, time to learn, or effort to use. The costs for the tasks we do often are much less important than the costs for rare tasks. We will pay more money for a can opener that we use daily than for a wine opener that we use once a month. But if we drink a lot of wine and open very few cans, our calculation will be reversed.

In products that assist with tasks that are performed very frequently, the value to the user is quite high. So those products can carry considerable learning costs. For rarely performed tasks, the product needs to be low cost. But remember that cost involves not just price, but also ease of learning and ease of use. Any product that is easy to learn and easy to use has some room on the cost side for price.

This is a little abstract, so let me give you an example. To complete the task of opening a corked bottle of wine, you need to engage in three steps: Remove the seal at the top, then insert the corkscrew, then tug it to remove the cork. This first step can be annoying. You have to get a knife and poke it in and tear off the top flap of the seal, leaving an irregularly shredded ring around the wine bottle opening.

But there is a device that does this for you called a foil cutter. You simply put the top of the wine bottle in its mouth and twist, and it removes the foil perfectly every time. These devices, which look to me to cost about $1.00 to make, sell for $7.95 to $9.95. If you open a bottle of wine every night, that price is a bargain. If you open a bottle of wine once a week, it is still a bargain. If you only pop the cork once a month, is it a bargain? It certainly isn't if you have to find and read the instruction manual each time you use the device or if you have to remember which side of the device is up or if you have to remember where you put it the last time you used it. But this device is very easy to learn and very simple to use, so its cost is actually pretty low and its net utility is pretty high.

Let us look at this graphically.

Products in the upper left of **B** in Figure 5–1 have very high utility at very low cost. This is where you want your products to be. The lower right of the **D** quadrant is death. It represents very low utility and very high cost. Let us look at Figure 5–1 to illustrate that point.

The diagonal line is the dividing line for net utility. To the left of that line, net utility is strong. To the right of it, net utility is weak. Where you put your innovation in relation to that line is a guess. Where your customers put it is the deciding factor for whether your product succeeds or not.

Figure 5-1.

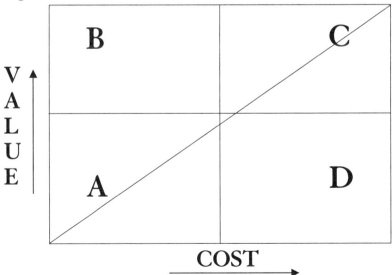

Reinventing the Picture Hanger

Now let's go back to sorting through the steps in hanging a picture. We are looking to do several things. First, we want to look for steps that can be eliminated entirely. Second, we want to look for steps that can be combined with other steps. Third, from the list of steps that can be eliminated and the list of steps that can be combined, we want to select those items that collectively constitute the "sweet spot"—the group that represents the highest net utility. This is the place where we will get the most bang for our buck. We may not stop there, but that group will form our core product.

Let us take another look at our list:

1. Collect pencil.
2. Collect hammer.
3. Collect picture hanger.
4. Collect measuring tape.
5. Determine rough horizontal location.
5. Determine rough vertical location.
7. Measure the distance from the ceiling to the top of the picture.
8. Add to that number the distance between the top of the picture and the center of the stretched picture wire.
9. At your rough horizontal location, measure down from the ceiling to the height indicated by your calculation in Step 8.
10. Place a mark.

11. Measure horizontally from a reference point such as a wall to set your exact horizontal location.
12. Place a mark.
13. With your measuring tape, draw a horizontal line from your horizontal mark across the imagined line of the vertical mark.
14. With your measuring tape, extend a line from your vertical mark across the horizontal line.
15. Nail your picture hanger at this intersection.
16. Erase the remaining pencil lines.
17. Hang the picture.
18. Replace the pencil.
19. Replace the hammer.
20. Replace the measuring tape.

Immediately, you will notice several things. There are some steps that you really cannot eliminate. For instance, Steps 15 through 17 look like they are there to stay. But then you will notice that there are several steps labeled "collect" or "replace." Those steps imply that each item is kept in a separate place. If they were all in the same place, we could replace seven steps with two. We can do that. We can create a small kit that includes a measuring tape, a variety of picture hangers, a small tack hammer, and a soft pencil with a built-in sharpener.

We have innovated the Handy Household Hanger Kit. That's great, but take a look at the steps that are left after you take those five out and ignore the ones that cannot be removed. That is the hard stuff: all that measuring and line drawing and the like. That is where the sweet spot will be found if there is one because the pain is not in collecting and replacing the tools. The pain is in getting the measurements right. As it is, doing the measurement tasks properly often requires two people. If you can take that out of the equation at low cost and include it in your Handy Household Hanger Kit, you may just have a serious product.

However, it does not seem likely that you can replace or remove the measuring. After all, location is the essence of the task. So we are stuck. Or are we? No, we are not, because we remember our Sherlock Holmes. In his 1892 short story "The Adventure of the Beryl Coronet," the great logician says, "It is an old maxim of mine that when you have excluded the impossible, whatever remains, however improbable, must be the truth." So, with Holmes as our guide, we will do the improbable and eliminate the measurement.

There are actually several ways to do this, and before I give you mine, let me give you one clue: It is the measuring that we want to eliminate, not the placement on the wall. That is, we still want the picture to be centered between two windows and the center of the picture to be at adult eye level, but we do not need to know that on this wall that means 22.25 inches from the ceiling and 42.875 inches from each window sash. The precise measurements are really not relevant to what we are trying to accomplish in most cases. Only the relative location matters.

So, if only the relative location matters, we can do this fairly simply. Give yourselves a few minutes to think this through. Then I will give you my solution, not because it is the right solution, but because it is one of the possible solutions and using it will allow us to see how many steps we can eliminate with simplicity and thus how much net utility we can generate.

GO

This is an interesting problem, and if you dislike hanging pictures, you may find it even more interesting because you have something to gain from the solution. Let us look at the sample solution and see how it works.

Picture a device about two feet long and about two inches high and an inch thick—pretty much the shape of a level. It has a rod sticking out of each end. In the center of this rectangle are four things. There is a level bubble in the exact center on the top edge; below it is a crank that moves the rods just described. At the bottom of the rectangle is a hook just like a picture hook in which there is a hole about three-fourths of an inch up on its shank, just where the nail would go in a picture hanger. At the top center is a sliding bar (like the bar at the top of the device they measure your height with at the doctor's office) about six inches long. The two rods telescope; each is six feet long when fully extended. They move in opposite directions simultaneously when you turn the crank.

The device looks something like Figure 5–2.

Assume that this device is added to my Handy Household Hanging Kit, and that to place my picture, I do the following:

1. Collect the Handy Household Hanging Kit.
2. Hang the picture from the hook.
3. Adjust the sliding bar so that it touches the top of the picture.

Figure 5-2.

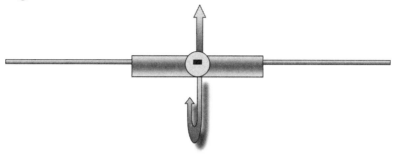

4. Remove the picture.
5. Place the device against the wall so that the top of the sliding bar is at the height where I want the top of the picture to be and the device is roughly centered between the two windows.
6. Crank the rods until they are touching the two window frames simultaneously. Now the picture is exactly centered without any measurement.
7. Put a pencil through the hole in the hook shank to mark it.
8. Nail the hanger at that mark.
9. Hang the picture.
10. Replace the Handy Household Hanging Kit.

I have a total of 10 steps instead of 20, and these steps are a lot simpler than all of that measuring. That is my impression, anyway. But only the customer's impression matters, so we cannot determine if we have hit the sweet spot.[1] However, we know we have reduced the total number of steps by 50 percent, and we have made the most difficult steps simpler to execute. Perhaps the approach itself is too complex. But customer research will tell us that. Short of that, on the face of it, there is high net utility here, assuming that the sale price is reasonable. If the market agrees with that assessment, then we have innovated in a task that people have been carrying out since the Middle Ages. It's not sliced bread, to be sure, but it's no small trick either.

A Quick Recap

Before we move on, we should recap this chapter, which contains a good deal of important information.

Once we have decided what tasks a product is really used for (Step 1), we must then break down those tasks into steps— one verb per step and one object per verb. We then need to review and analyze the steps, looking for steps that can be removed or combined and, in particular, looking to eliminate steps in such a way as to most increase the net utility to the customer. We then need to select the "sweet spot" steps and find a way to combine or eliminate them. Once we have done that, we need to validate our concept with the market to ensure that the market sees high net utility in our innovation. If it does, then we are ready to start building the new product.

Innovation Workout 2: It's Midnight on Christmas Eve

I am not a good present wrapper. Indeed, I suspect that under a Christmas tree piled high with unlabeled wrapped packages, any relative of mine could pick out the ones I had wrapped with just a glance. They are the ones with nine layers of tape, misshaped ends, jagged edges, and a Post-it note instead of a fancy label. So I need some help in wrapping packages, and I have come to you for it. I would like you to come up with an approach for wrapping presents that is simpler and produces better results than the current approach. I will make the task simpler by telling you that I almost always give books as presents and that those books fall into only two categories—normal-sized hardbacks and trade paperbacks, which tend to be slightly smaller in all dimensions than normal-sized hardbacks and slightly larger than regular paperbacks.

Your first step will be to write out the steps involved in wrapping a book. Next, you will want to combine or eliminate some of those steps. Finally, you will need to account for the two different sizes of books involved as well as minor variations within each of those two sizes. The product you invent will be sold only in bookstores.

Do not cheat. Do not propose something like a fancy bag to stick the book in. Those can be bought now. Your task is to replicate the conventionally wrapped book by some unconventional means. And be sure to remember net utility. If the process takes an instruction manual to understand, then it is probably not a process that customers will flock to in great numbers. Painful as the current approach is, they already know how to wrap packages. They won't read a book to learn how to do it a new way.

Chapter 6

Making Innovation Happen

Step 2 inherently raises an important point. Assuming that you buy into the ideas that tasks matter more than functions, that tasks can be broken down into steps, and that steps can be analyzed and then combined or eliminated, how do you go about implementing this?

There are two approaches to this problem: process and culture. I favor culture (a term I will elaborate on shortly), but I recognize that process has some allure. The issue is far from decided, and there is enough weight in each camp to make it worthwhile to summarize the arguments and let you decide for yourself. We do need to be careful to limit the process argument to "innovation through process," however. This is the idea that one can create a process that will yield innovation in some mechanical way. This is the notion that one can build an innovation "machine" with interchangeable people that will automatically produce brilliant new products. The idea that you can take the human factor out and still create innovation seems like the ultimate bureaucratic fantasy to me.

That fanciful notion can easily be confused with "innovation through organizational structure." As to that concept, I think there is little room for argument. It is possible to organize in such a way as to foster innovation. Indeed, that is one of the subjects of Chapter 11.

There is also a danger that a rejection of the idea of innovation through process would be seen as a rejection of the idea that methods can lead to innovation. That would also be a mistake. Methods such as the one in this book provide a means for coming up with innovative product ideas. Methods can work in either a culture-oriented business or a process-oriented business. The ideas will still be generated in both. But how they will be handled and whether serious innovation will be fostered equally in both environments is a serious question. We can organize and operate in ways that promote innovation, and we can do so in ways that inhibit it.

With these distinctions in mind, we will begin by looking at the process approach.

Process

Systematizing all aspects of the organization will always be management's objective. That's why they call it management, not supervision or something else less action-oriented. Managers want to manage things. Management takes place through process. Managers cannot be everywhere and see everything, so they hold weekly staff meetings, require monthly reports, provide templates for approval, establish individual goals. and the like. All of this makes sense if you are running a factory or a sales force, but it is less clear to me that this is an appropriate approach where innovation is concerned.

There is an anonymous management aphorism that states a basic problem:

> The objective of all dedicated employees is to thoroughly analyze all situations, anticipate all problems prior to their occurrence, have answers for these problems, and move swiftly to solve these problems when called upon. However, when you are up to your rear end in alligators, it is difficult to remember that your initial objective was to drain the swamp.

The more one is involved in day-to-day reporting, budget planning, meetings designed largely to allow the uninvolved to feel involved, and other structured activities, the less time and energy one has to devote to the more reflective and intuitive activity of innovation. You lose the ability to focus on the future because the present is overwhelming you.

Implementation, it is said, drives out planning.

The most successful project I ever worked on was one where the innovation took place during the sale and change in management of the company. Such periods tend to bring normal activities to a halt for a while, and that was what happened here. During the hiatus, a group assembled informally to work on a vexing problem and came up with a paradigm-changing solution. A colleague in that project years later was asked to do a presentation on it as a case study in innovation. He described the environment at the time and announced, quite honestly, that the only lesson he could draw from the experience was that if you wanted to innovate, put a lot of smart people in close proximity to each other, but don't give them enough to do.

That is not a theory that is likely to endear itself to cost-conscious management. Management will look for a process that leads to innovation that has specific allocated resources and measured deliverables. It will want the innovative proposals delivered on a certain date, in a certain format, with the appropriate PowerPoint template used.

Much as it galls me, and much as it contradicts the notions discussed earlier regarding implementation driving out planning, there is something to be said for this approach and for the idea that the methods described in this book can be applied in that environment. Let us take a look at how that might work and then go through the advantages and disadvantages.

In a process-oriented structure, each product line has an innovation goal. This approach is familiar to many of you because it is the 3M or Procter & Gamble approach, where expectations are set regarding revenue generated by new products. In truth, all companies do this, whether they realize it or not. At some point in their planning process, they look at next year's overall revenue goal and figure out how much of it can reasonably be achieved through new sales of existing products, acquisitions, and price increases. That combined growth is subtracted from the revenue goal for the year, and whatever figure is unaccounted for has to come from new products.

The product line management then creates an ideation process to generate new ideas. The methods described in this book could be used to aid in that ideation process and should produce results. The next step would be a filtering process for the concepts developed in ideation. That would typically involve a higher-level group whose role would be to set performance thresholds and approve and prioritize projects. And that is where things run into trouble, because such a process has a tendency to drive the level of innovation down to a lowest common denominator. Let me explain.

First, process-driven cultures are inherently risk averse. You put in a process to systematize, to reduce the variables, to narrow the risks, to eliminate surprises. When we talk about "thinking outside the box," the box we are talking about is the process itself. When micromanagers start talking about thinking outside the box, someone needs to stand up and say, "We have met the enemy and he is us."

Second, the central goal of this process is short-term revenue. The chief question in the minds of management is, "How do we most economically achieve the next year's revenue goals with the highest likelihood of meeting those goals and convincing our bosses that we are reliable (and also making our bonuses)?" If that is the mindset, then incremental innovation is the course that is most likely to be followed. If last year we made $1,000,000 by introducing a new line of metallic-finished faucets, then this year we should go for pastels. If our round-shaped toaster sold well in 2006, then let us add a round bagel toaster in 2007. No one can argue with doing more of the same when "the same" made you money last year.

But, at some point, "the same" becomes self-parody. Look at razors. The old adage is that you are not selling razors, you are selling blades, because the profit is in the continuing sale, not the original one. Razor manufacturers are faced with a real dilemma in their fight for market share in a commodity business. You would think this would make them a hotbed of innovation. But what we have seen over the past decade or more is an advanced form of more of the same. First razors went to two blades, and that was interesting. Then they went to three blades; it was still a product that one might switch to. When razors went to four blades, people began to make jokes about it. Now they are at five blades (with a single "trimmer" blade on the other side because the five-blade razor is too unwieldy to be used in nooks and crannies), and you have to wonder if these folks can come up with an original idea or if they just need to face up to the fact that what they are selling is now a fully innovated product and that the competition will be based on price. At some point you need to recognize that, as Freud said, "Sometimes a cigar is just a cigar." If you cannot change it fundamentally, then you have to do something else.

The "something else" will be dealt with when we turn to Step 3. But our immediate problem is how to innovate in an environment that puts a priority on short-term revenue needs, where product development is focused on one year out and the powers that be are willing to "gamble" only on sure things.

The answer is to turn to the customer. If you have answered Step 1 correctly and have responded to Step 2 with a smart analysis and a reduction of steps, and if that reduction of steps is in the "sweet spot," then you have a proposition that yields high net utility. If that is the case, then even a prototype will knock customers out. They will not need marketing to convince them. They will not need a long sales call to win them over. They just need to try it.

If you can demonstrate that customers are dying to buy this product, then you ought to be able to sell it to management. If customers are dying to buy it and management cannot see its way to funding it, then there is no hope. Either you are deficient in selling or management is totally clueless (or both). In any event, a company that is unable to react to strong customer demand for a product is a company that has lost track of its customer, and there is not much to be done in such an environment because there is nothing that is harder to change than culture. Which brings us to the next option.

Culture

As mentioned earlier, a later chapter deals in depth with optimizing an organization for innovation. To a large extent, that chapter really discusses how to foster a culture of innovation. So that material will be dealt with then. This section is intended to explain why a culture of innovation is more powerful and productive than process-driven innovation—innovation as part of the planning cycle.

These remarks apply primarily to large organizations. Small organizations do not have the same types of problems. To start with, it is important to understand that all large organizations are dysfunctional (although, to borrow from Tolstoy, each is dysfunctional in its own special way). Of necessity, such organizations are all deeply matrixed, and every intersection on a matrix is a potential point of dysfunction. The more intersections there are, the more likely it is that breakdowns will take place. That is not criticism. It is mathematics.

This means, as every good manager knows, that at some point management cannot actually manage. It cannot direct the day-to-day activities of thousands of people, especially when it wants to encourage ideas moving up the ladder as much as it wants to enforce directives moving down the ladder. What it can do is provide monetary incentives, motivate emotionally, and make certain favored paths smoother than others. It can hire innovative people and reward innovation itself. It can "brand" innovation as a major part of the corporate ethos.

It can also choose *not* to do those things and send the implicit signal that innovation does not matter to management. It can reward implementation instead and send the reverse signal that day-to-day functions are valued more than innovations. And that can be a very legitimate strategy if, despite what you will learn from Step 3, you conclude that your business is in a permanent commodity state. If that is so, then ruthless efficiency in execution is your primary goal, because you are competing on price, and thus you must keep costs to a minimum to protect your margins.

There is a lot to be said for the cultural approach.

1. It creates a positive and cooperative environment in which employees feel empowered to innovate and can learn to do so from their colleagues. The process approach more closely resembles a command-and-control model—a negative model and not a fertile ground for innovation.

2. It opens up product innovation to all employees, not just a select few in Product Development. That allows people with natural innovative talent to rise to the top, no matter what department they started in. It creates a natural talent scouting environment that is more accurate than any preemployment test is likely to be.

3. It is self-sustaining. In fact, it is more than that: It creates its own growth. It does not need to be managed as much as it needs to be steered.

4. It creates more ideas than can be used. That allows the process lovers to winnow through the extra ideas for those with the proper amount of whatever accounting measurement is fashionable that year. This means that it can resolve both short-term and long-term needs.

5. It creates bolder ideas. It allows innovators to stretch beyond the sure thing into the high-risk/high-reward concepts.

It is fair to say that the companies that build innovative cultures are the companies that do the most and best innovating. Procter & Gamble, 3M, FedEx, Toyota, Rubbermaid, and the rest of the innovators did not get to be centers of innovation year after year because they had the best business case review processes. They did so because the company cared about innovation, the management cared about innovation, and the employees cared about innovation. You just do not get that in a process-driven environment. The primary goal in a process-driven environment is complying with the process, meeting the hurdle rates, using the right templates, and juggling the numbers to get the "right" result.

It is, of course, possible to compromise. One could have a process for ordinary product proposals and a different approach for more radical innovations. One can designate a pot of capital for higher-risk/higher-reward options. You can have one structure for annual new product needs and another for long-term game-changing product innovations.

Unfortunately, with this approach, the long-term path is always in danger of being cut or underfunded. It takes tremendous discipline and courage to think and fund the long term when the short-term numbers are hurting. But failure to do that will always exacerbate problems downstream.

That bifurcated approach, if sustained against the day-to-day needs for capital to make next year's plan, can raise product development above the plain vanilla level. But it does not do much to promote an innovative environment, and so, while it may provide an avenue for approving and developing bold ideas, it does not itself foster bold ideas.

And innovation is always bold. It is not more of the same. It is not product line extensions. It is not putting the chrome on. It is always a leap of the imagination. In Chapter 7, we will look at Step 3 and see that bold innovation on one task is only a stepping-stone to real game-changing innovation.

Chapter 7

Step 3: Taking It to the Next Level

WE HAVE COME TO THE LAST, AND POSSIBLY THE MOST RE-warding, question. Before we jump into it, let us review the first two steps.

> Step 1: What task is the product really used for?
> Step 2: When I know what task a product is really used for, are there any steps that I can remove from that task?

By responding to these two questions, we have changed the focus from the function of the product to the use of the product. We have aligned our product with the customer's task, and we have made our product perform as efficiently as possible in executing that task. What more can be asked of us? Haven't we fully met customer expectations?

Yes, we have. If we have answered the first two questions correctly and executed well, then we have a customer who is probably very satisfied with the product, and maybe even impressed. That's great, of course, but it is not enough to stay ahead. To stay ahead and to have the customer be not just impressed but bowled over, we need to do one more thing: We need to take the customer to a place where she did not expect to go. And we have to do that first. We have competitors who are watching our every move. Unless we can patent some concept, they can stay very close to us without creating a single new idea themselves. Ultimately they can match us at the point when the product settles down to the commodity level.

This is the moment when the Step 3 becomes important. Step 3 assumes that it is entirely possible to break away from a commodity attitude and take a startling leap that will leave the competition in the dust.

The Promised Land

Here's an example of the type of product idea that the third question can lead you to.

You've just come off a flight on one of today's crowded and amenity-free airplanes. You've waited for your luggage for a very long time. You've waited in line for a cab to take you to your hotel, and the cab has struggled through city traffic jams to your hotel. You enter the hotel lobby, and what do you see? You have arrived at the same time as some convention, and the check-in lines are 20 people long. You've got a meeting in an hour followed by a dinner, and then you're off on another flight in the morning. There is nothing you'd like more than to have 30 minutes of peace and quiet, but the line is crawling along. Your entire day is now in ruins.

Then you see it.

In the lobby, there is a kiosk for checking in. You move in quickly and insert a credit card. Your name comes up, and in just a few seconds a key is presented to you. You are very relieved, and you have a newfound respect for this particular hotel chain. You are smiling for the first time all day. Then you notice that the screen on the kiosk is flashing a new message. You read the message and your smile turns to a grin. You may even giggle a little. You spend another couple of minutes at the kiosk, go to your room, and vow to stay only at this chain from now on.

What did the screen say to bring out this kind of reaction? Did you win $1 million for being the millionth guest? Were you upgraded to the Presidential Suite?

No. The screen simply said, "We notice you are checking out tomorrow morning. Do you need a boarding pass for tomorrow?" If you said yes, then it provided access to the online check-in sites for all the major airlines and printed out your boarding pass for you. The kiosk exceeded your expectations dramatically because it not only took care of your current task (checking into the hotel) well, but it also recognized an adjacent task that you might wish to complete and facilitated its completion. It did so seamlessly from your perspective, and you saved time and anxiety.

And that leads us to:

Step 3: What tasks are the very next tasks that the customer will want to perform after using my product?

This question is important for two reasons. First, it leads us to product ideas that are going to make our customer even happier. Second, it leads us to new product lines and thus extends our business into new areas. Not only do we win the customer for our core product, but we can also add new products and new customers to our business.

It is a little bit tricky but important to remember that tasks are different from steps. In Step 2, we spent a lot of time breaking down a task into its component steps. Generally speaking, steps are not useful in themselves. When someone hangs a picture, he does not say, "I completed the measurement task; now I can take a day off." The task—the goal, the end state—is to hang the picture. When that is done, the task is completed. When I complete a measurement, I have not completed a task; I have merely completed one of the steps necessary for completing the task. The distinction between a step and a task is important. Customers know that they want to complete tasks efficiently, so they demand the elimination of steps.

On the other hand, customers may well not connect different tasks, even though they are often linked in time. Checking into a hotel one day and getting on a plane the next day are consecutive steps on my itinerary and in my mind, but truthfully, I do not expect someone else to connect them for me. So when someone connects seemingly disconnected tasks for customers, those customers are not just pleased, they are surprised and delighted, and rightfully so.

Some examples may help.

1. We have already seen what happened with the hotel check-in kiosk. The two tasks of checking in and getting a boarding pass are not connected physically until we experience the connection at the kiosk. But when we do experience that connection, it is powerful, and it stays with us. We do not connect the two tasks physically because they are quite different tasks, but they are related to each other in time. Someone who checks into a hotel for one night is very likely to be traveling the next day, and that travel is likely to be by airplane.

2. Microsoft is much maligned, but it does some very clever things, and these things have become so much a part of our lives that we tend to overlook them. One of the clever things that Microsoft has done is the "Send To" function in many Office products. At one time, when we completed a document in Word, we had to close the document, open up Outlook, open a new e-mail, click Attachment, browse to find the document that we just completed, and attach it to the email. The "Send To" function allows us to do that with little more than a single click, and thus it both reduces steps and connects discrete tasks.

3. Machines for kneading dough have been around for a very long time. Ovens for baking bread have been around for a long time. But bread machines combined the two tasks into one, and that unleashed a commercial dynamo. When the bread machine was invented in 1987, more than 1 million bread machines were sold in the first year, even though units cost several hundred dollars.[1] Taking kneaded dough, putting it in a pan,

and placing it in the oven is not a huge task, but the joining of this task with the task of kneading dough yielded hundreds of millions of dollars of revenue in just the first year. And that was just the beginning. Amazon carries 186 cookbooks for bread machines as well as 112 different bread machines, and your local grocery store probably has two or three dozen prepackaged bread mixes just for such machines. This is now a huge business, and all it does is combine two seemingly separate tasks into one.

4. We all know that coffee is big business these days. I work in a building that has the highest-volume Caribou Coffee outlet in America in it. This is despite the fact that the company provides free coffee about 25 feet from the Caribou entrance. The lines at Caribou can be daunting, but there is never a line for the free coffee. This penchant for high-quality (or, at least, high-priced) coffee has started to affect the home kitchen. Coffee grinders began to be common in kitchen stores in the 1980s. Espresso machines reached home appliance departments in the United States in the 1990s. More recently, the two have been combined, and there are now dozens of espresso machines that will grind your coffee beans and deposit precisely the right amount of freshly ground coffee in the receptacle for brewing. Many machines also are self-bleeding, which is a Step 2 innovation, since it eliminates a step in the coffee-brewing task.

5. Sometimes you want to put things in a box for storage, and sometimes you want to put things in a box for shipping. If you wish to ship something, you have two

tasks. First, you pack the object. Second, you ship it. To pack the object, you go to your local office supply source and get a box, some packing materials, and some tape. Then you return home and pack and label the box. To ship the package, you go out again to the post office to mail it. But Mail Boxes Etc. connected these two tasks. You can bring your object there, purchase the box and packaging materials, package it on the spot (or have the store pack it for you), and hand it in for Postal Service or UPS delivery. The first store opened in 1980, and now there are 5,600 locations. And all they did was connect two tasks.

6. A person goes into a CVS Pharmacy with a high fever. She wants relief from the symptoms as soon as possible, and she is seeking over-the-counter drugs as the fastest way of doing that. But as she enters the door, she sees a Minute Clinic, one of dozens opened in CVS outlets. The clinic is staffed by a nurse-practitioner who is authorized to prescribe certain drugs. So, instead of buying an over-the-counter drug that will mask her symptoms, she spends five minutes in the clinic, receives a prescription for a strong antibiotic that will cure the problem, walks over to the pharmacy counter, and fills the prescription. The customer will probably also buy the symptom-masking products to provide relief until the antibiotics kick in. Instead of just masking the symptoms, she has started the cure and has done so in just a few minutes. She has completed what she perceives as two different tasks in one place and at one time and is very pleased to have done so.

7. One of the most successful and examined innovations of the past 25 years is the Post-it note. Sometimes we write a message and there is no need to secure it to anything. We put it on someone's chair, or we place it in a folder or an envelope. However, sometimes the note does need to be secured because it is also serving as a marker in a book or a reminder that must be kept in a visible location. This second task was traditionally completed with Scotch tape or the like.[2] But Post-it notes combined the tasks of note writing and note securing into one task.

8. You are mowing your lawn. It used to be that this task was followed by the arduous task of raking and bagging the clippings. But your lawn mower has a bag in the back that collects the clippings for you and facilitates moving them to lawn bags for disposal.

9. You are having a dinner for two, and you open a bottle of wine. You put in a pourer so as not to have the wine drip. Then, after dinner, there is half a bottle of wine left, and you need to recork it. So you take out the pourer, put it away, find a wine stopper, and insert it. But the Velevet wine pourer/stopper is a single product that does both tasks well.

Contiguity, Loose Linking, and Leveraging

Notice a few things about these examples.

First, the tasks are contiguous. That is, a person doing the first task is very likely to do the second task, and to do so very soon after doing the first task. Contiguity can be either functional or temporal. Functional contiguity takes place when one task is related to and follows another, such as the bread maker example or the coffee grinding and brewing example. Other tasks are temporally contiguous. While the tasks themselves seem separate, the one usually follows the other. The hotel kiosk, the wine pourer/stopper, and the clinic in a pharmacy are examples of this type of contiguity.

Second, the tasks are loosely linked. You do not have to buy the drugs from CVS. You do not have to bake the bread in the machine. You can bake it in the oven instead. You do not have to send your document to Outlook. You can go to Outlook or some entirely different e-mail program, open an e-mail, and attach the document then. You do not have to buy the shipping box from Mail Boxes Etc. You can pack the goods at home, and the company will still ship it for you. And so on. But you can choose to take the linked route, and it is easy for you to do so.

Loose linking is a very important concept. There is a natural inclination to build a product that will do everything. However, such products tend to be doomed. There is very interesting research on this subject.[3] The research reveals that people will buy a product because of its *abilities*. That is, presented with five different VCRs, users will tend to purchase the one with the most features. But product satisfaction is based on *usability*. Owners of a product that does everything are often dissatisfied with it because they find it too complex to use. The array of features that made the product attractive is often impossible to learn or, once learned, to retain in memory. So, the owners either do not use the product, use only some of the features, or go out and buy a simpler version.

This complexity arises because the product is optimized for one primary task (playing a VHS tape), and then the other features are stuck on the product in a less than optimal way. Let us look at an example.

John Jones buys a VCR. His primary task is to play prerecorded tapes. But every now and then he wants to record a show on tape and send a copy to a friend. To achieve this goal, he has two main choices. First, he can buy a VCR and try to set it up every now and then to record a show. If John is older than 15, he will find this part very difficult because the VCR maker has spent most of its effort on the main task of playing prerecorded tapes.

The alternative is to obtain a digital video recorder such as TiVo. Such products are optimized to record shows off the air. So the task of recording is simple, but these machines do not record directly onto VHS, and they cannot play a prerecorded tape.

The answer is to have two machines: one to play VHS tapes and to record them, and the other optimized to capture content directly from the television. The loose link is to build a function in the TiVo machine that says, "Send to VCR." Then all that is required is a simple cable connection between the two machines and you have the best of both worlds with minimum complexity. Of course, this is all just a variation on the concept of net utility.

Third, for the most part the tasks leverage each other. That is, if each task independently is well executed, the temptation to take advantage of the convenience of joining them is very high, even if one task could be done better elsewhere. If my bread machine kneads bread well *and* also bakes the bread well (even if not as well as an oven), then the convenience factor will outweigh the perfection factor most of the time. There may be times when I want a thicker crust, which bread machines generally cannot supply. Then I just remove the kneaded dough and proceed in a regular oven. The linking is loose, so I can do that. But when the tasks are both performed optimally, even though they are loosely linked, customers will be willing to pay a premium for the convenience that even loose linking brings. If Mail Boxes Etc. costs me 20 percent more than buying boxes and packing material at an office supply store, I will nonetheless buy the materials from Mail Boxes Etc. because of the convenience factor.

Contiguity, loose linking, and leverage constitute a breakaway from traditional "tool" product development. When we build tools, we optimize them for a single task. When we link tasks properly, we create workflow solutions that both improve our customers' productivity and also make our relationships with those customers stickier.

Take a look at Microsoft Office for a minute. Office creates an environment that allows us to "Send To" e-mail and other Office applications. It allows us to "Cut" from one application and "Paste" into another. It provides an Excel functionality ("Insert a Spreadsheet") in a Word application. There is much room for improvement in how it does these things, but there is much to applaud in Microsoft's creativity in including these features. They all stand as evidence of an understanding that, while each task must have a tool that is efficiently designed for completion of that task, one task often leads to another, and bridging the gap between the two is a powerful product idea.

Contiguity, loose linking, and leverage are important factors that affect sales and marketing as well as product development, and their interactions with those areas make them key to the successful launch of an innovative "task-to-task" product.

Linking Tasks and Changing Business Models

A review of those interactions will be helpful. Let us say that you are in the prepackaged bread ingredients business. You sell boxes of flour and yeast and salt and other ingredients that, when combined with water from the customer, will yield dough for, say, rye bread. Your sales and marketing groups are focused on reaching grocery stores, where these products are traditionally sold. However, if your company goes into the business of making machines that knead the dough or that knead and bake it, you will need to redirect those efforts or create new sales and marketing arms because kitchen appliances are a hard sell in grocery stores. It may be worth your while to do so. You may also be in the coffee business, and you may see an opportunity to create and sell "grind and brew" coffeemakers as well. These also will require a different marketing and sales channel. But the decision to divert sales and marketing resources to a different channel is a serious one that requires real analysis. Will the business really come out ahead if you do this? Can your brand, which is associated with prepackaged bread ingredients or coffee, be extended to include machines that use those products? If you fail, will it hurt your brand equity in your traditional line?

If, on the other hand, you make dough-kneading products, adding a "knead and bake" product to that line will actually leverage your existing sales and marketing efforts because they are already directed at the small appliance market. So in connecting tasks, it is vital that an analysis of the impact on sales and marketing be conducted. A brilliant product with one foot in each of two markets is a product that may be difficult to turn a profit on.

And loose linking may provide your marketing people with the opportunity to partner with someone else to create the perfect task-to-task offering. This is essentially what the hotel chain did in the example of the boarding pass kiosk. It linked its service (online hotel check-in) with somebody else's service (online airline check-in). The link was not really anything more than a handoff to another web site run by an airline. A hard link would have taken the customer's name, entered it in the airline check-in screen, and linked that name to a frequent flyer number. That would have required registration for this "service," and probably would have required that the customer remember a password and user name.

But the loose-linked customer gained nearly all the advantages that a hard-linked customer would have found, and did so with less pain than a registration process and the "memorize the password and user ID" activity would have required. The customer can obtain a boarding pass by typing in a few words and his airline authentication code. An additional password is not needed.

This is not much different from what happened when you called an airline in the "old days" (1999 or so). When you finished making your reservation, the airline reservation clerk would ask you, "Would you like to book a rental car or hotel for your trip?" The airline itself did not have hotels or rental cars, but it had relationships with companies that did. The customer received a convenient hotel or auto reservation, and the airline received a commission from the hotel or rental car company.

Of course, in some cases it would be better economically to own both tasks. But that will not always make business sense. If the second task is so remote from your core business that entering the new field would detract from what you do best or require massive investment in a market that you are unfamiliar with, it is probably best to partner. But, if this is done properly, both partners will gain synergy as a result.

The great thing about task-to-task innovation is that the opportunities are everywhere and are easy to locate. All you have to do is look and ask.

Let us say that you make eyeglass cases. What could be more of a commodity product than that? But if we take a look at what users do with an eyeglass case, we find that they do two things: They put their glasses in it, and they take their glasses out of it. If we take a closer look, we will see that when they take their glasses out of it, it is very likely that they will also clean their glasses. To do this, they may have stuffed a glasses-cleaning cloth in the case. You could very easily include a pocket for such a cloth and the cloth itself in your eyeglass cases. People also often clip sunglasses on top of their prescription glasses, but there is no place to store those clip-ons in an eyeglass case. But you could change that quickly. Now you have an eyeglass case that contains a pocket containing a glasses-cleaning cloth and a clip to hold the sunglasses. No one else has either. Suddenly your product is not a commodity anymore. You are the market innovator. You can establish brand equity and distinguish yourself from the "me too" pack. And it cost you practically nothing. Both of these features come from simple, everyday observations that you can literally do at home. The market research cost for ideas like these is zero.

But that will not always be the case. You cannot always observe your customers interacting with your product and then observe what they do next. The next best thing is to ask them.

Let us move you back over to the bread maker business. Between 1985 and 2005, you made a lot of money because your machines combined two tasks. But you made most of that money in the first five years or so, when the market had few competitors and the price point was high. On Amazon. com today there are 112 bread-making machines for sale, and some cost less than $50. This is no longer a business where great margins are easily obtainable. You may even be calling it a commodity business. But it is not. Your customers still have some inconveniences in their efforts, and you can innovate if you know what those are.

But you cannot put your market research team in your customers' kitchens for hours at a time. Even if you could, the presence of the researchers would skew the results.[4] So instead, you ask a group of people to fill in a diary about their bread making. You ask them to write down each step they take, and then to write down the three things they did next after the bread was finished, even if they think those things were totally unrelated to the bread.

Some people will be better than others at reporting their own actions, but if enough people write down their actions, you will find that several product innovations will emerge from their collective responses.

For instance, some users are likely to report that the next thing they did was to take out a grate to put the bread on so that it can cool. You can easily add a slide-out grate to your product. Others will tell you that one of their next steps was to get out a storage bag and put the bread in it. You can add a storage bag container to your product. Others may tell you that they put the bread machine away. Well, you cannot do that for them, but you can try to make your bread machine occupy a smaller footprint so that, perhaps, they will not feel the need to put the machine in storage. This smaller footprint will be an attractive sales proposition in urban environments where apartments are small and kitchen space is at a premium.

Again, this is very inexpensive research. There are no focus groups. No market surveys. Just observation and reporting. Understanding reality is the highest form of market research; artificial environments such as focus groups come in a distant second. Focus groups can be very useful once the concept is fleshed out. They can tell you about reactions to small details, and they can be especially helpful in positioning your product. But idea generation and idea validation are the products of real observation under circumstances that are as real as possible.

Step 3 completes our basic set of innovation tools. These tools are simple and effective, but they still need to be used with care, and the answers we provide for these questions need to be constantly revalidated with customers. The product developer needs not only to know that an idea such as the cooling grate for bread makers facilitates a common task. She also needs to know that the customers put a value on the addition, and she needs to decide that the addition does not introduce too much complexity to the product. The notion of net utility is the ultimate filter for product innovation.

Chapter 9 in this part will sum up the entire process and provide a detailed outline on how to incorporate it into your product development. But, since it is only an outline, it does lose some of the subtle points along the way, so please do not take it as a complete roadmap. Before we get to it, however, we will look at how this process relates to services.

Now for our third innovation workout.

Innovation Workout: Your Midterm Exam

By now, you think you have this thing figured out. We will test that with several innovation workouts. Each one is a relatively simple task-to-task concept, so you should try to tackle them all. Once you have given your answer, see if you can find an opportunity to observe the actual behavior and decide whether that observation validates your idea or, instead, suggests some new approaches. Or, better yet, observe first and then come to some conclusions. (Sample answers to these questions are provided in Appendix A, but there are no "right" answers—only wrong ones and good ones.)

A. *Going to the movies.* A couple is in line to buy tickets at your movie theater. They get to the cash register and order two tickets for *The Monster that Devoured Cleveland*, and then you warmly surprise them by . . . ?????

B. *Parking the car.* You own an airport long-term parking concession. It is typically crowded, and customers typically do not return for three days. A customer comes to your lot, pushes the button on the ticket machine, and is delighted to learn . . . ?????

C. *Caller ID.* The phone rings at home, and your caller ID system tells you that your son, who has just moved, is calling from his new number. You are very pleased with your caller ID provider because . . .?????

D. An e-mail arrives from someone you have not previously received e-mail from. You read it and respond to it. Your e-mail program takes things one step further by . . . ?????

E. Look around for other examples of task-to-task product innovation opportunities. You will find them everywhere. Practicing this will sharpen your observation skills, and that will sharpen your innovation skills.

Chapter 8

Spotlight on Services

Up until now, we have largely been talking about goods—products in the sense of tangible things that people buy and use. But everything that has been discussed thus far applies to services as well. We just need to understand that services either are single tasks or connect related tasks. In either case, services are increasingly important.

The world economy is rapidly changing from one that produces hard goods to one that produces digital goods as well as services of all sorts. In 2006, three-quarters of the U.S. workforce was employed in the services industry. The services industry itself is enormously complex. My corner automobile repair shop is performing a service. But so is Verizon.

Some services are very simple in scope. A simple service is one that exists in isolation from other services. Dry cleaning is normally a simple service. When we go to a dry cleaner, our task is to get our clothes cleaned. It is not part of some more complex activity. Similarly, sewing and upholstering are simple services. Such services are also essentially the same things as tasks. The service provider takes a task that we cannot do or do not want to do and, for a fee, does it for us. So if we are not skilled in upholstery, but we have a chair that needs work, we take that chair to an upholsterer, who does the job for us.

If we want to talk to someone on the other side of town, we could put up telephone poles and string some wire, but it is a lot easier (and ultimately less expensive) to contract with Verizon to provide that service for us.

Services and Tasks

A service business is a business that takes a specific task that we have and does it for us. It is a means of outsourcing tasks.

In terms of our approach, that means something quite specific, something that simplifies part of our analysis. Step 1 (What tasks is the product really used for?) is generally answered by the very definition of the service business itself.

If we need a chair reupholstered, we have a task. If we could do upholstery ourselves, we would do it. But because we cannot (or do not want to), we pay someone else to do that task for us. Service businesses acknowledge the task the customer wants to complete, understand it well (or they will not stay in business for very long), and allow their customers to substitute someone else's labor for their own in completing the task.

Now, it is possible for a service business to confuse its function with the customer's task. A computer repair shop owner could think of his business as simply a way to monetize his hobby of playing with computer hardware. When you bring your PC in to be fixed, you want it back as soon as possible. But the owner could be intrigued by your particular configuration and want to keep it a while longer to explore its possibilities. This, too, would be a short-term business, and it is a fair generalization to say that service industry businesses know their customers' tasks and are competent at completing them.

Simplifying Services

Because service businesses themselves answer the first question, we can quickly turn to Step 2 (When I know what task a product [or service] is really used for, are there any steps that I can remove from that task?). Now we are on familiar ground, and this is a place where many service businesses may not have trod. Service businesses are labor-intensive and so are very cost-conscious, but at a gross level that simply means being careful about the number of employees they have and their wages and benefits and seeking to optimize those costs. It does not mean that they are efficient in their use of these expensive resources.

If you follow your own day-to-day experiences with service businesses, you will quickly agree. It was not until very recent times that banks and airlines (sophisticated service businesses) had a single line for customers to wait in, as opposed to expecting them to gamble on one of several lines. Many restaurants still have the person who takes the order (a relatively expensive employee) bring and remove the dishes as well.

Many service businesses are too small to have much division of labor (although they may be wrong about that, since outsourcing is a form of division of labor), but many that are large enough fail to take advantage of such tactics. Service businesses can go further than they have, and Step 2 will help them to do that.

The challenge in Step 2 is to list all the steps involved in the completion of a task and to eliminate some of those steps. But that is a little more complex in services businesses than it is in hard products if you wish to go beyond simple wage and benefit analysis. When you talk about eliminating steps in service businesses, ultimately you are often talking about eliminating jobs. But there are other approaches. In fact, there are three ways to eliminate steps in services or otherwise make them more efficient:

1. Work harder.
2. Work smarter.
3. Automate.

Working harder is not within the scope of this book. I can find many people who would claim that I have no expertise at all in that area, so I will not pretend to give advice here. Working smarter and automating are within its scope, though. So let us look at an example and see how we would answer Step 2 in a service industry model.

Any service industry will work, but we will stick with upholstery, and our model will be a one-person upholstery shop. Here is a list of steps for an upholstery project:

1. Initial contact
2. Upholstery selection
3. Style decisions (e.g., Will there be piping? Will decorative nails be used?)
4. Pickup of furniture piece
5. Reupholstering
6. Return of the furniture

A core fact here is that in this situation, the most expensive labor (that of the skilled reupholsterer) is being used to do a lot of fairly mechanical tasks. So working smarter may mean getting cheaper labor to do the less-skilled tasks. It may involve outsourcing the pickup and delivery of the furniture or offering a discount for customers who do that work themselves, for instance. It may involve some third party opening a service business for the service businesses by serving as the pickup and delivery company for many upholstery shops. This would allow the skilled craftsmen to take in more business, reduce the price for existing business, or to take home a higher percentage of the revenue from the business.

So, we can work smarter and make some progress, but there is not a lot of room for automation in reupholstering, is there? Perhaps there is.

The decisions in Steps 2 and 3 (upholstery selection and style decisions), could be narrowed or even actually made without the involvement of the skilled craftsman. In that sense, they can be automated. Online selection of fabrics or mailing of swatches can be combined with the making of key style decisions through an online form. Mockups of the resulting look could be displayed online. The craftsman could also be available by phone or e-mail for consultation if that were necessary, but some substantial portion of the decision-making process could be made in the home where the furniture will appear, without the craftsman traveling to the home and spending an hour observing the decision-making process.

Even if these steps save only one hour of time, both the craftsman and the customer benefit from that, so the same service can be provided at lower cost and higher margins, and the craftsman can take in more work.

So, by focusing on the steps and looking for an opportunity to work smarter or to automate, we can turn a service business that is competing on price and its reputation for quality into a business that can produce the same quality at a lower price while doing a higher volume of business. That approach distinguishes this business from the 40 others just like it in the Yellow Pages. It is better for the owner of the business, and it is better for its customers because it delivers more net utility.

Joining Adjacent Services

That takes us through the first two questions. But to get to Step 3 (What tasks are the very next tasks that the customer will want to perform after using my product [or service]?), we need to look at more complex services because their very existence means that the third question has not been adequately answered in the sectors in which they operate. As we shall see, that is so because if the third question had been answered, then the services would no longer be complex.

To answer the third question in the services world, we must step back and see past the silos that services have stuck themselves in. Just as the first question is easier to answer in a service environment, the third question can be quite a bit harder—but very rewarding when it is answered.

The complex services businesses—which include such things as financial services, legal services, real estate transactions, health care, insurance, and the like—are different in many ways from hard goods such as faucets and intermediate goods such as software. And they are very different from simple services.

The complex services do not exist in isolation. All service businesses sell an actual result, as opposed to something that can be consumed or used. They sell the completion of a task, the consummation of a goal. Complex services can do that too. They can provide a specific result. But that result may take the customer only part of the way to the completion of her task. Complex services cannot always provide the final desired result—the end task—by themselves.

They can provide part of that result. A bank sells accounts and financial instruments designed to safeguard or grow one's money. It also sells mortgages and other forms of credit. A real estate broker sells either the marketing of a home or access to the market for homes (through the Multiple Listing Service and acquired knowledge), depending on which side of the transaction the broker is on. A lawyer sells knowledge of the law and the ability, by license, to represent parties in court.

People often go to these professionals (and to others like them) because they want to achieve some specific and simple result. They want to earn interest on their savings. They want to sell their house. They want to incorporate their own business. Achieving each of these results is itself a task, very much like the tasks involving hard goods and software that we have discussed throughout this book. So one would think that it is quite possible to take the three questions we have outlined and apply them to the services industry. And it is possible—but there is a hitch.

Complex services are intertwined with other services. Normally, no one service provider can produce the desired result. The service of one entity needs to be linked with the service of another. This tends to confuse the task/function distinction.

The threshold requirement is the first question itself: What tasks is the product really used for? You have to determine what the task in a particular situation is. But the businesses in the complex services industry have mangled this notion beyond all imagination. They have divided the real task into all of its components (its functions), scattered them to the four winds, and then put up barriers between them so that they cannot easily be combined. But do not take my word for this; let us look at a perfectly ordinary task and see how the services industry has reduced it to its least efficient method of execution with relatively little coordination involved.

Your name is Jones, and you want to buy a house. Millions of people do that every year. It is a task, and people think of it as a single act. But in order to buy a house, you will have to deal with multiple players in the services industry, each of whom serves a different function. Here is a partial list of the functions you will find yourself involved in so that you can complete the one task:

1. Contract with a real estate broker.
2. Obtain a mortgage from a bank.
3. Hire an inspector to evaluate the property.
4. Hire a surveyor to have a survey done.
5. Obtain mortgage insurance.
6. Obtain property owner's insurance.
7. Hire a lawyer or title company to conduct the closing and record the sale.
8. Hire a tax accountant to deal with the tax consequences of the purchase.
9. Arrange for movers to transport your furniture.
10. Get insurance to cover the move.

During the course of this transaction, you may also deal with the seller's broker and the seller's lawyer as well. And, with a slight variation such as a sale by an estate or the need for a zoning variation, you can add several other folks to the list as well. Each of these people will be in a different location, operating on a different schedule, and with overlapping, but not coordinated, information needs. Each will charge you for her services. You will not have the time or information you need to bargain over those charges effectively.

There are lots of problems with this scenario. It is dysfunctional and inefficient. It is annoying and exhausting. It is utterly unnecessary. But for our purposes, the main problem is that it totally hides the task. Ask each one of these service professionals what he is doing, and you will get the following answers:

1. *Real estate broker:* Selling the Smith house (*not* helping Jones to *buy* a house).[1]
2. *Bank:* Making a loan.
3. *Inspector:* Looking for defects.
4. *Surveyor:* Measuring a lot.
5. *Mortgage insurer:* Selling mortgage insurance.
6. *Property insurer:* Selling property insurance.
7. *Lawyer:* Reviewing documents and supervising the signing.
8. *Tax accountant:* Preparing taxes for filing.
9. *Moving company:* Moving furniture.
10. *Moving insurer:* Insuring goods that are in transit.

Not one of these people will say, "I am helping Jones to buy a house." But that is all Jones wants to do, and she is footing the bill for this laundry list of services. Each service provider is essentially telling Jones that he does not care what *her* goal is. He has a role, and he has blinders on where everything else is concerned.

While this is an extreme and somewhat exaggerated example, it is not the only example. If I want life insurance, I may need to have a physical performed by a doctor. If my parents die, I will need an undertaker, and I may need to deal with property appraisers of various sorts, accountants, lawyers, and insurance agents. My task is to deal with the consequences of my parents' deaths, but the service industries related to that task are not aligned to it or with each other.

If my arthritic knees are bothering me, I go to the doctor, who sends me to a specialist. The specialist sends me to an x-ray facility. The x-ray gets read by a radiologist, who reports back to the specialist. The specialist gives me a prescription, which I take to a pharmacist. The pharmacist contacts my insurance company. If it balks, then I may have to contact my employer's HR department or engage a lawyer to sue the company. If it pays, then I still have to submit a claim to my tax-free health savings account to cover the copayment or deductible. This is a genuine mess.[2]

One can argue how much of this mess is the fault of the components of the services industries and how much of it is caused by artificial lines being drawn between related sectors by government or by the professions, but that argument is endless because in some instances the sectors themselves have pushed hard to create and enforce the artificial lines. They profit from the structural inefficiencies because the buyer has little opportunity or room to bargain with each of a dozen service providers, as she could and would do with a single, unified service provider. So while it would be fun to play the "blame game," it is more useful to play the innovation game and put these folks out of business. Because at the end of the day, what matters is that the customer is not being served efficiently, and that means that the opportunity for innovation exists.

So, to begin to apply our approach in a services context, we first need to dig through this underbrush and figure out what our customer's task really is. We cannot let ourselves be distracted by the dysfunctional nature of the services industries involved. That means we need to talk to customers. They have the clearest vision on this.

They will not say, "I need to have a survey done." They will say, "I want to buy a house."

They will not say, "I need to make a copayment of $10 on my prescription." They will say, "I need to do something about my aching knees."

They will understand exactly what their task is, and their frustration over the fact that not a single one of their service providers really has the same goal as they do will be great. No one is actually getting paid to put Ms. Jones in a house. Each provider is getting paid to complete some aspect of that task. They are all indifferent in a financial sense to the ultimate goal of the customer.

Indeed, to some degree, they have no stake in that customer at all. If Ms. Jones does not buy the Smiths' house, Mr. Williams will. The property will not sit vacant eternally. If Ms. Jones does not buy the Smiths' house, she will buy another house somewhere down the road. So this customer with this one task is a commodity to the service providers. She may be treated well. She may get excellent help. But her actual goal is immaterial to the service provider, so the provider has no incentive to make the overall task less onerous. The provider is focused solely on his function—which is exactly the wrong place to be focused.

Here let us look at a simple analogy. It is 1910, and we want to get into the automobile business. We set up the business as follows:

1. We get an order for a black sedan.
2. We order a frame from Company A, and we have to describe the specifications.
3. We order a seat from Company B, and we have to tell that company what it is we want.
4. We tell the headlight company to send some chrome headlights.
5. And on and on and on.

We would quickly be out of business because you cannot proceed efficiently if you treat each aspect of your product as unique and isolated from all others each time you build the product. Someone with uniform standards and established procedures who orders parts in advance to a standard part description will eat your lunch for you. And so he should.

In a complex service situation, the need is to join the tasks—to give the customer the opportunity to select a package deal. The participants in the package deal need to pass from one task to the next the necessary information to complete the task, just as a bumper is passed along the assembly line.

But remember what was said in Chapter 7 about such

linking: It needs to be loose linking. If you try to solve the real estate problem by building a monolithic structure that handles all aspects of the task in one uniform way, you are jamming a solution down the customers' throats just as much as was the case when the different tasks were kept separate from each other.

Loose linking simply means what is referred to in software as open source. If you are a real estate agent (the usual entry point for property buyers), then you are in the driver's seat. When a buyer comes to you, you can say:

"Okay, if you are dealing with me, then I have a system that points you to one bank, one title company, one insurer, and so forth."

In that case, the buyer has to risk monopoly pricing to obtain a more convenient transaction. On the other hand, you could say to the buyer:

"Okay, if you are dealing with me, I have a system that allows you to input your data and get bids from three banks, three title companies, three insurers, and so forth. And I will take care of passing the core information to all of these folks and presenting you with a unified bill."

This type of linking, which allows the customer to choose the best of breed and to do so efficiently, is both cheaper and more efficient. It also saves money for all of the participants because they do not have to start their part of the transaction in isolation from the numerous other players who are gathering and using the same information.

Better yet, what happens if the entry point for the buyer is not the real estate agent? What if the agent is just one of several services offered by a "buyer's manager" who works only for the buyer for a specific fee? That person engages a broker, arranges for a mortgage, handles the closing, and so forth. These people represent scores of buyers and so can negotiate discounts on all aspects of the purchase and have no conflict of interest. Their incentive is to hire the best people at the lowest price, and that matches up exactly with the buyer's needs. They present one face to the buyer, and that is what the buyer really wants—linked services.

So, while linking services is great, linking them in a way that maximizes customer value is even greater.

Loose linking is done in many instances now. Chapter 7 mentioned the hotel check-in kiosk that also provided me with my boarding pass for the next day's flight. Go to Expedia or Travelocity or Orbitz or any of the other online travel services, and the service will get you a flight, book you a hotel, get you a rental car, and so on without your having to travel to multiple sites and enter the same data each time. And the service will offer you multiple choices in each category.

My cable company now bundles phone, cable TV, and high-speed Internet access into one package, but I can bundle them any way I want, so that if I choose to get satellite TV, I still get the bundling advantages for the other two services. The company I work for has a health insurer who also manages the health savings account. Because of the insurance claim, the insurer knows what deductible or copayment I have paid, and it automatically sends me a check for it from the health savings account. This is a nice loose link. It will be doing even better, as far as I am concerned, when it sends the check directly to the pharmacy, so that I do not have to lay out the cash to the pharmacy and deal with the $10 check, but it has come quite a long way. And it has saved money by reducing paperwork, and has made me a happier customer as well.

The complex service world abounds with such opportunities to look at the adjacent tasks and connect them. The movie theater innovation workout at the end of Chapter 7 illustrates the situation perfectly. There, even a single business in the service industry actually puts a brick wall between the different products it sells (food and entertainment), institutionalizing inefficiency. If you have looked at the sample answer to that workout in Appendix A, then you know what that means.

A visit to a computer repair shop provides another example. The PC is left for a new hard drive, but the customer realizes a bit later that the keyboard needs a simple repair as well. But when he calls the shop, he is told that the keyboard repair group is another department and that he will have to deal with that department separately.

Walking through a detailed example may help illustrate the point.

Americans are constantly losing weight. And, apparently, they are also constantly gaining it back. How else do you explain the massive diet industry? But if we take a close look at this activity, we see inefficiency and opportunity.

Again, we start with the steps:

1. Learn what your dietary needs are in terms of calories, fats, food groups, and so forth.

2. Look for recipes that support those needs and are attractive.
3. Create a list of meals for a certain period of time.
4. Create an ingredients list.
5. Shop for those ingredients that you do not have at home.

The first step requires us to go to a nutritionist or some other information service. For the second step, we will have to go to a cookbook or some other recipe source and look for meals that meet our needs. Special diet recipe sources may make our task easier by providing a list of healthy recipes, but we still have to correlate that information with our specific dietary needs. We have to do this multiple times for multiple meals. Then we have to create a consolidated ingredients list, and then we have to do the shopping.

That is a lot of work for a week's worth of dinners. It is a lot of work, though, only because the various services we have used are isolated from each other. That isolation is unnecessary and unprofitable. Various diet companies have figured this out and have disintermediated all the other service providers by delivering quantities of frozen diet dinners at extremely high prices, and they have made a lot of money doing just that. But they provide only a limited menu of food that is not fresh. And so it ought to be quite easy to disintermediate them right back. However, the isolated services have not taken the steps to do that. Here is an example of what they could do.

The new dieter goes to a web site run by a grocery chain.

It allows her to input her dietary needs for a day and her preferences for various foods. It asks how many meals are desired, and for how many people. It takes that information and presents a list of recipes. The user selects the ones she wants. The web site then offers a list of ingredients with a check box next to each. The user checks the ingredients she needs and then clicks a button for delivery. The groceries come to her. A task that might eat up two or three hours has now become a 20-minute task.

Each step in the process just described can be done independently today. You can go to a web site and find recipes. You can look up dietary information at another web site. You can print out a list of ingredients, recipe by recipe. You can order groceries for delivery online. But you cannot do all of this as part of one activity and through one source. And that (as the various frozen diet meal providers have found out) is what you want to do.

To achieve the customer's goal, you must understand the customer's task, and here it is to efficiently cook a set of meals that will help you to be healthier. It is not to look up recipes. It is not to measure calories. It is not to prepare sets of ingredients, and it is not to go to grocery stores. Yet that is how the services are set up and run, and that is what they optimize to.

Are the people who run service businesses like these idiots? No. But their business and their brand and their expertise are all associated with one function. Any other function is, to use the catchphrase of the timid, "beyond their core competency." That phrase is a classic example of corporate narcissism. Customer needs determine a business's competencies, not its executives' image of what the company is in business to do. IBM's core competency was building main-frames. Xerox's core competency was building copiers. And one can bet with absolute certainty that when personal computers were first being sold, someone at IBM said, "This is not for us—our core competency is mainframes."

This inward-looking posture prevents these businesses from seeing the business the way their customers see it. They see only their function, and they align their business to that function. But very often their function is simply one piece of a complex puzzle (a real estate transaction, for instance) that the customer must get through in order to get to the next piece of the puzzle. Getting past the bad guys and getting to the next level may be fun in video games, but it is not fun in the real world. It is inefficient.

The solution, again, is observation. When your company sells a rug-cleaning service, what else do your customers want to do? Might you have customers who want their windows cleaned or their soot removed or their ducts cleaned? If you are in the business of photographing children, might your customers also want framing and mailing services? If you sell burglar alarm services, can you also do mail forwarding for customers who have an alarm because they spend half the year in Florida? Can a plumber and an electrician get to-gether and offer a broader range of homeowner services?

The list is literally endless. But then, so is the opportunity to innovate. To get back to the lessons of Chapter 1, all busi-nesses need to align to such opportunities, and that is just as true of service businesses as it is of businesses selling tradi-tional products.

Chapter 9

Putting All the Pieces Together

THE PREVIOUS EIGHT CHAPTERS CONTAIN A GREAT MANY elements. These chapters present a plan of action for enhancing your product innovation activities. In this chapter, the goal is to put those action elements together into a comprehensive plan that can be easily and inexpensively implemented.

This chapter does not substitute for the previous eight, though. The examples and elaborations and workouts in those chapters are there to train you to use this chapter. Reviewing those chapters, especially the chapters containing the questions themselves, is a good idea. In particular, reviewing the workouts and making up some more of your own will be helpful because these mental workouts provide the training that will make the difference between good innovations and great innovations.

This plan will work, but there is one condition.

The attitude of the people working on it must be entirely customer-focused. If the approach is: "What notions can I best apply my marketing skills to?" or, "What concept is our technology group best suited to deliver on?" you may get a great marketing plan or you may get a product that is efficiently built, but marketing and technology do not buy the product—only customers do. And there is no reason to believe that what is good for technology or good for marketing is good for customers.

The process presented in this chapter has several parts, and there is some discussion of each part. Then, at the end of the chapter, an outline of the parts with the discussion removed is given, to serve as a handy guide.

Let us begin at the beginning, then.

Part 1: Gather the Facts

Remember Step 1, *What tasks is the product really used for?* This is the very heart of the process, and it is a question that must be answered factually, not guessed at. Customers surprise us. They use products in ways we do not imagine. In our kitchen, we have a product put out by Saran called QuickCovers. These are easy-to-use, disposable covers for bowls of any size. In truth, they are nothing more than disposable shower caps put to another use. I do not know how Saran came up with this concept, but my suspicion is that the idea probably appeared in a *Hints from Heloise* column, submitted by someone who had no idea she was spawning an industry. I hope so, anyway, because if you want to get a daily dose of practical innovation, there is no better source than Heloise.

This shower-cap-as-bowl-cover, of course, is the reuse of a product, not the creation of a new one. But, if my theory is correct, it originally came from observation of customer behavior through the medium of a newspaper column.

And customers surprise themselves. If you asked a hundred customers what are the tasks done by a kitchen faucet, you would get very few complete lists, and you would get a good many answers that focused on the function of the faucet—the delivery of water into the kitchen.

So gathering the facts really means two things:

1. Ask customers what they do with the product.
2. Observe customers directly.

As noted, customers will not always be able to describe the tasks they use a product for accurately and clearly. But you need only one right answer. If you ask a hundred customers, the odds are pretty good that a few will be good enough self-observers to tell you what it is they do with the product in a task-oriented and useful way. Failing that, some will tell you part of the story, and others will tell you another part. Among all the answers, there will be enough useful descriptions to allow you to form a hypothesis that can be tested through observation.

An example will help here. If you ask someone to describe what she uses a snow shovel for, you may get several different answers. Eighty of a hundred people may say, "I use it to shovel snow from my walkway." But five may say, "I use it as a large dustpan after sweeping my driveway." And two others might add, "I use it to remove ashes from an outdoor fire pit." All of the answers are true, but each of the uses is different in substantial ways. Together, they mean to you that the task of a snow shovel is to remove unwanted materials from a hard surface. The different specific uses may suggest that three different products are needed and that you can fill the gap suggested by these make-do uses of the snow shovel, or they may suggest a modification of the core product to make it more useful for the less frequently mentioned tasks.

You may find one user who describes all possible tasks precisely and accurately, but it's more likely that you will find a piece here and a piece there.

Once you have asked customers what they actually use the product for, it is a good idea to test the answers. It is quite possible that they have left something out or that you will observe something in how they do the task they have described that can help you to understand how the product can be improved to make the task more efficient.

Take the snow shovel example. If you watch someone try to sweep dirt from the driveway into a snow shovel, you may observe that the angle of the shovel itself is an obstacle to completing the task. A snow shovel with a deep curve to it will not work because when the bottom edge is flat to the ground, the dirt will fall right out again after it is swept in. When the snow shovel is used to clear the ashes from the fire pit, some ashes may fall off the side of the shovel. These pain points in the tasks are your opportunities for innovation.

Observation is best carried out in person. Sometimes that is easy. Workers in a factory can be observed. You can invite a hundred people into a test kitchen to observe them making a cake. Purina, the pet food company, maintains an animal rescue facility where the reactions of pets to food innovations can be directly observed. But not all tasks will lend themselves to such a format.

Substitutes include videotaping and log keeping. The former is considerably more accurate, but the latter is less intrusive. Some combination of the two, such as videotaping a few people and asking many others to write down their steps and their issues as they go, is probably an optimal solution.

The key point is that your answer to the question in Step 1 must be fact-based. It cannot be an opinion. There is no exercise more futile or more ironic than a group of product development people sitting around arguing about whose opinion of customers' behavior or desires is correct. Opinions do not matter at this point. Facts about customers do matter.

Part 2: Answer the Question in Step 1

If you have done Part 1 diligently, then this part should be easy. If you put five people in a room and give them the same simple set of facts, the odds are pretty good that they will answer Step 1 in the same way. But, if you give them something more complex—if you tell them that a person who owns a hose uses it to spray water directly on plants and connects it to a sprinkler to apply water to grass, but then you add to that list the use of the hose to help wash the car—the answers may start to vary and may be only roughly similar. You may hear "transport of water" or you may hear "delivery of water under pressure," and these statements may be intended to mean roughly the same thing.

But roughly is not quite good enough. The answer to this question is at the heart of everything that will follow. If you miss by an inch, it is like a rocket heading for the moon that is an inch off at launch. By the time it gets to the moon—well, it won't get to the moon. It will get someplace else—eventually.

So the answer needs to be specific or it will not do you any good at all. But how do you get a specific answer for a multiuse product? Well, you do not. Think back to the faucet example. One of the chief learnings there was that what the manufacturer sees as a single product with a single function, the user sees as different products with different tasks. It is only when our answer to Step 1 matches the user's perception that we can match the product to the task. So when we see the kind of answers that we got on the hose question, then we have two choices: Ignore the different uses that we know exist and create a one-dimensional product that performs the most general functions of a hose, or heed the users' statements and see if we need to produce two different kinds of hoses.

There is a simple process to achieve that end. It requires us to list the tasks for a given product at their narrowest level. Every separate use should be treated as a separate task, using the same "one verb, one object" approach that we used in Step 2. For example, using the hose again:

1. Water bushes.
2. Water trees.
3. Attach to sprinkler.
4. Attach pressure nozzle and wash window screens.
5. Attach pressure nozzle and wash car.

Once we have done that, then we can look at these micro-tasks and ask, "Can I create a product that optimally fulfills more than one of these needs?" If the answer to that question is no, then we can stop right there and design five separate products. If the answer to that question is yes, then we need to connect these tasks. That would lead us to a new list of tasks at the second level that might look like this:

1. Water bushes and trees.
2. Water lawn using sprinkler.
3. Wash car and window screens using pressure nozzle.

At a third level, we might say that the attachment activities with the sprinkler and the nozzle might be the same thing, and thus we would have only two products to deal with:

1. Hose using an attachment
2. Hose not using an attachment

We have gone from five tasks to two products. But we have to be careful that we do not go too far. You can slice the onion too thin or too thick. What we need to find is the level of distinction that is meaningful to end users. There is some art to this. It is sometimes theoretically arguable what the end task is. But the simple way to deal with that difference of opinion is the way to deal with all differences of opinion in product development—ask the users. It is only their opinion that matters.

So, now we have examined the customer's actual behavior and we have determined a meaningful set of tasks from that behavior. The next part involves converting what we have learned into greater efficiencies for the customers who buy our products and the new customers we would like to attract.

Part 3: Answer the Question in Step 2

Recall that Step 2 asks: *When I know what task a product is really used for, are there any steps that I can remove from that task?* We spent a lot of time in Chapter 5 going through this process, so you should have a pretty good grasp of it. But another illustration will help. We can use our hose example again to restate the point.

There were three tasks for the hose:

1. Water bushes and trees.
2. Water lawn using sprinkler.
3. Wash car and window screens using pressure nozzle.

Ideally, our hose will do all three of these tasks and do them in the most efficient way possible. One thing is immediately obvious: The hose should have an easy way of adding a nozzle or a sprinkler and a simple way to switch between those two attachments. We need to start a list of potential product innovations, and the first two items on that list will be:

1. Easy on and off for nozzle or sprinkler
2. Interchangeable connectors for nozzle and sprinkler

That was easy. But we are far from complete. Before I could do any of these tasks, I had to get the hose from storage of some sort and connect it to the faucet. Then, when I am through, I have to drain the hose, disconnect it, and return it to storage. So now I add to my list of potential product innovations:

3. Easy-access storage of the hose that also allows for draining
4. Easy connection to the faucet

Now I have four product ideas designed to reduce or simplify steps in the task. Perhaps these are all great and original ideas (gardeners will know that they are not), but they are not great because I thought of them. They are great only if customers agree that they have net utility. And that takes us to the next part.

Part 4: Validate Product Concepts Through Net Utility

You now have a list of product concepts that make sense to you. If you have been careful in your work, there are probably some sound ideas included in the list. But that is not certain, and you do not know which of these ideas is best. That requires customer validation. To get this, we need a measure of net utility. And to get that, we need to do a little research.

Let us look again at the chart we used in Chapter 4.

Please rate this product for each statement on a scale of 1 to 5, with 5 meaning that you strongly support the statement and 1 meaning that you do not support the statement.

	1	2	3	4	5
This product would, in balance, make my life much easier.					
This product would look good in my house.					
This product is unlike anything I have seen before.					

All that this requires is a simple prototype or a Power-Point mock-up. What you are trying to find here is customers' initial impressions. More traditional (and much more expensive) market research tools can help you work out the fine points of the product and gain insight into the pluses and minuses from a positioning perspective. But this simple and inexpensive approach can help you to validate your ideas and place your bets among competing ideas.

The truth is, it can be even simpler than this. The one

thing the chart does not really measure is emotional intensity. The ratings on the 1-to-5 scale may be simply a rational reaction to the product or to your pitch. So getting the information in a conversation with a customer while observing her reactions directly may tell you more than having 100 people fill out the form. There is a big difference between a product that people really like once they figure it out and a product that people grasp and want immediately. The first type of product is not too bad, but the second is a home run.

Part 5: Answer the Question in Step 3

Step 3 asked: *What tasks are the very next tasks that the customer will want to perform after using my product?*

This question is relevant in two circumstances:

1. You have an existing product that has become a commodity, and you want to bring some life back into its margins by bundling it with something new. For example, you sell propane and the gas itself is a commodity, so you bundle it with a QuickTank service model to add new life to it.
2. You are launching a new product that is similar to, although somewhat superior to, other products on the market. Here you add to that base product a product that facilitates a related task to essentially create a new market. The old products were one-task products.

Yours is a two-task product. The bread machine is a good example. Prior to its invention, lots of people sold machines that did the task of kneading dough. The bread machine baked it as well and made the knead-only machines irrelevant overnight.

Under these circumstances, the linked product reenergizes a commodity market or establishes a brand new territory by displacing existing products in the same market.

Part 5 requires you to observe customer behavior carefully. The examples at the start of Chapter 7 and the workouts at the end of that chapter will help train your mind to make the correct observations, but practicing every day is enormously helpful. Wherever you are and whatever you are doing, look around. What do you do after you take out a can of soda? You open it by pulling the tab. But you used to open it by going to a kitchen drawer, taking out a can opener, using it, and then returning the can opener to the drawer. Someone observed this inefficiency and changed it and created an industry.

The next thing you do with your soda might be to put ice in a glass and pour the drink. This used to mean opening the freezer, taking out an ice cube tray, removing some ice, refilling the tray, and returning the tray to the freezer. Now it means putting the glass in the ice dispenser in your refrigerator door and filling it that way.

If you watch carefully, you will find half a dozen examples every day, and you will be able to apply these day-to-day observational skills to your work activities as well. The kitchen is a very good place to start. Net utility really matters in kitchens, and you will find its applications in product linkages everywhere in that room.

Part 6: Product Approval

This material will be covered in Chapter 12, so there is no need to go over it in depth now. The essential point is that the three steps outlined here provide a very useful way for management, even if far removed from day-to-day customer interactions, to judge whether proposed products have a customer focus and are likely to be well received in the market.

The Short Guide to Innovation

Part 1: Gather the Facts

Observe customers closely. Videotape them. Interview them. Ask them to fill out diaries. Get as much factual information about their behavior as you can.

Part 2: Answer the Question in Step 1

The question here is: What tasks is the product really used for? You have to get this one right. Everything else depends on it. State hypotheses and challenge the hypotheses of others until you are sure you have nailed this one.

Part 3: Answer the Question in Step 2

The question here is: When I know what task a product is really used for, are there any steps that I can remove from that task. Write out the steps involved in the task. Use one verb and one object per step. Several people should make lists and then compare them and argue them down to a single list. Then look for opportunities to eliminate or combine steps.

Part 4: Validate Product Concepts Through Net Utility

Use the net utility matrix and a simple survey to start the validation process.

Part 5: Answer the Question in Step 3

The question here is: What tasks are the very next tasks that the customer will want to perform after using my product? Answering this question requires more observation. Hone your observation skills through daily practice.

Part 6: Product Approval

Management should use the questions here to ensure that the products it approves are customer-focused and will create new demand.

PART 2

The Context of Innovation:

People, Management, and Organization

Chapter 10

The Human Factor

THERE ARE ONLY THREE THINGS NEEDED FOR INNOVATION: a method (such as the three steps provided here), an organization that promotes and takes advantage of innovative concepts (as will be discussed in Chapter 11), and the people to do the innovating.

People drive innovation, whether it is based on process or on culture. And, while the three steps described here can be applied by almost anyone, they and every other approach to innovation will yield greater success when the people using them are themselves more innovative. But, that having been said, there are two types of innovation, and the people needed for each are different.

We tend to thing of innovation as *BIG*, operating on a

grand scale and changing markets, leapfrogging the competition, and sending the stock price soaring in a single bound. It can be that, of course. The assembly line—a process innovation—made automobiles affordable for millions of Americans and so not only created profits for the Ford Motor Company, but also changed the American economy. The iPod took Apple's stock from 14 to 85 (notes a man who sold at 29). Google's innovations in searching and its creative business model created more than $140 billion in shareholder value in just a few years.

But innovation can also be *small*. It can take the form of incremental improvements in routine activities. Each small innovation may be barely visible and may save only a relatively small amount of money or add a relatively small amount of value to a product line. However, the sum of these miniature innovations repeated across hundreds of processes and dozens of product lines can be staggering.

Both forms of innovation thus add considerably to the value of a business. But the innovators in each instance are quite different.

The *big* innovator has, to some degree, genius. She can see things that no one else can see. Big innovators take dozens of isolated pieces of information and see a pattern in them. They view a problem in a way that others have not viewed it. They find attributes in a product that others have not observed. They see opportunity where others see the status quo. They are born, not made—but they can be found, and they can be nurtured.

The *small* innovator, on the other hand, can be created. The skills involved are teachable and can be greatly enhanced through the creation of an environment that values innovation. And businesses are wise to put some focus on these people because their innovations both add value to the business and increase their own job satisfaction.

Because big innovators are born that way, we will ignore them for the moment and deal with them in Chapter 11. Here, we will deal with small innovators.

Teaching Innovation

To decide how to enhance innovative skills, we have to know what those skills are. I will list several skills that I think are crucial to innovation. There are certainly others.

Observation. Innovators need to see things as they actually are, but not be bound by the present state. They must observe critically. They must have the ability to look at the processes and products they see every day with insight based on the goal of each process or product. We are better off with people who can see clearly than with people who can think clearly if we have to choose between the two skills. Great observers are rare birds, and their observations can be converted into product innovations by others. But without their observations, even great minds will not add much.

Curiosity. This skill is closely related to observation. The observer must have a questioning mind. Why are we doing it that way? Would it make sense to try this?

How well is that working? If you are not curious, you will not come up with anything new. One strong indicator that someone is probably not an innovator is that the person has an encyclopedic knowledge of every aspect of the product and sees not just the trees instead of the forest, but the veins on the leaves on the trees. If you recall the folks who, in the early PC days, memorized hundreds of DOS commands and were deeply upset when Windows ultimately made their knowledge irrelevant, you will know who such people are. They become so enamored of their deep and arcane knowledge that they cannot see the faults in the product. Indeed, they may regard people who want to simplify the product as weak or lazy.

People skills. Real innovation typically arises from contact with and empathy with customers. You actually do have to feel their pain in order to understand the pain points of the product and remove them. That means that you have to get out among your customers and that you have to seek out the unhappy customers. You will not learn from the happy ones. You have to inspire those unhappy customers with confidence that you actually do care about their problems and that you really do want to solve those problems. You have to be able to hear really bad news and not be defensive. You have to hear that the product you poured your sweat into is not delivering value to the customer, and you have to be excited by the opportunity that this information provides to you.

Questioning. Innovators must have the mental and emotional skills to question what is going on around them. Questioning the status quo requires imagination and courage. But that questioning has to be something more than mere rebellion against authority, which is ultimately self-centered. It should flow instead from a desire to improve the business, to create more value for customers, or from the pure thrill of creating something out of nothing. Curiosity plus passion is an amazing combination.

Pragmatism. Innovators need to distinguish between the cool and the useful. The concept of net utility needs to be in their bones, or else they will fall victim to the merely cool. They have to be able to flip from the state of awe induced by a really good technological advance to the cynical mode of asking, "But what is the use case? What do customers get out of this?"

Action orientation. The best ideas in the world are of no value unless they are acted on. Doers are more valuable than dreamers. But dreamers are only rarely doers in the sense of carrying out the full implementation of a product from concept to first customer delivery. They usually have to hand it over to the detail people needed to execute the grand plan. However, they should have enough action and passion in them to evangelize the concept and to ensure that the implementers fully understand the vision they are being given.

Diplomacy. A good portion of managers got where they
are by being very good at doing things the way they
have always been done. They are implementers, and
their comfort zone is in converting old ideas into
products. Such people are often resistant to change—
to innovation. But once they are convinced of the
value of change, they can make all the difference.
Only Nixon could open up relations with China. Only
the manager who thoroughly understands the old way
can successfully introduce the new way. So the innovator needs to gain management support while not
threatening management itself. This requires diplo-
matic skills and starts with relationship building.
Treating the implementers as people who "don't get
it" is not a helpful approach.

All of these skills (observation, curiosity, people skills,
questioning, pragmatism, action orientation, and diplomacy)
can be taught to some degree, but in searching for small innovators, I would focus on the first four for two reasons: The
other three are general management skills that are not unique
to innovators, and the first four are less obvious and, I think,
more teachable than the others.

Big innovators are more of a challenge. They are rare and
hard to find—obscure mushrooms in a deep forest. But their
essential characteristic is creativity, and they cannot hide that.
They are funny or mercurial. There is a spirit in them that
needs to be let out. For that reason, they very often have an
artistic outlet that they are notably good at. You will find
them emceeing the awards banquets, doing skits at the sales

meetings, or penning subversive memos that get circulated around the building.

They may be discounted by their immediate supervisors because, if they are not engaged in creative work, they are probably not actually engaged in the work they are doing and getting paid for. Their performance review will say things like: "Very bright, but not adequately focused on the task at hand. Needs to spend more effort learning the mechanics of the job."

Assuming that you can find one or more of these special spirits, you still have to be a bit careful in moving them into a lead role in innovation. Not everyone with an innovative personality has all of the seven skills listed earlier. These people will by definition have skills in observation, curiosity, and questioning. They probably have people skills. They may lack diplomacy skills and they may not be action-oriented, but these can be compensated for by pairing them with someone who does have those skills.

That leaves pragmatism, and that is essential. The big innovator who cannot distinguish between the cool and the useful should be writing science fiction, not creating product ideas for customers. Innovators without pragmatism will waste your time and resources and will cause you to miss opportunities because you have followed them down a dead-end road.

There is a way to spot this failing, and it is through the use case. When you are examining a candidate for a big innovator position, the candidate should be able to propose innovative concepts, of course, but he should also be very comfortable answering the question, "What is the use case?"

First of all, the candidate's innovation should have a use case, and he should know it. If he cannot come up with a credible use case (even if you can), he does not care enough about the practical application of the product concept. Second, he should regard the use case as the supreme proof of the value of his concept, and so he should be delighted by the question instead of defensive about it. Finally, the use case should be at the tip of his tongue because his thinking should have started with the customer, not ended with taking the customer into account.

There will be more about the right people in Chapter 11, but before we get there, let us take a look at the people you want to avoid. These are the ones who can really waste your time and hinder your progress.

Innovation is very exciting work. True innovation actually does make the world a better place. It increases productivity, provides leisure, and reduces overall costs. As we discovered in Chapter 1, innovation drives successful companies. But innovation has a dark side: innovators in name only. They come in several types.

Innovators in Name Only

The Ladder Climber

This is the person who *has* to innovate because that is what management is demanding or rewarding. If innovation is this year's watchword, then this person will, by heaven, innovate. The ladder climber will come up with (or steal) a notion, dress it up in flash-powered PowerPoint, support it with the rosiest quotes from a focus group just as a bad movie has fabulous blurbs from negative reviews in its ads, and stare down anyone who disagrees with her. The odds that this person will come up with a genuine innovation are the same as the possibility that a broken watch is showing the right time: It happens twice a day, but it is merely coincidental. Ladder climbers are a true test of a company's adherence to accountability. If they get away with their act more than a couple of times, the organization is as much at fault as they are. Unfortunately, these people are usually fleet of foot and have moved to a new job or a new company before their old failings catch up with them.

The True Believer

The true believer has an idea that he passionately believes in. In fact, that belief probably goes back a decade or more. This idea is a "market changer," but every time it has been presented, management has failed to get it. The managers are "idiots" or, worse, "bean counters." The more open-minded true believer will occasionally fault himself for his failure or inability to communicate this breathtaking concept. Very often true believers actually do have an idea that constitutes a significant improvement. Where they often fail is by not seeing that the net utility is negative. The innovation takes too much effort to learn or money to acquire relative to the actual gain achieved. The true believers would use the product and be delighted with it, so it must be true that everyone else would happily go through the learning curve to take it up. They are early adopters themselves, and they believe that everyone else should be as well.

I had a product proposal presented to me once that had an enormous wow! factor to it—but that wow! literally would materialize only once every three years or so. The cost to the user for that innovation would have been about $700 to purchase and maintain the device during that period, and the user would have had to carry the device constantly. The price was too high. The only buyers would be those who were so blinded by the end concept that they ignored the cost of getting there. No successful business can be built around such customers.

Unlike ladder climbers, true believers are worth having around. They do generate new ideas, but they have to have someone around to filter those ideas for them. They see only the pot of gold at the end of the rainbow. They fail to notice that the rainbow can be reached only by climbing Mt. Everest.

Recyclers

Recyclers take yesterday's good innovation, change something that is incidental to it, and then call it new. It is a kind of raging "me too" syndrome that happens all over the place. A book comes out like *The Da Vinci Code*. It sells umpteen million copies, and within months eerily similar books begin to appear. A television show featuring forensics hits the top of the ratings, and not only does the competition imitate it, but it actually imitates itself by adding additional locales. I, personally, am looking forward to *CSI: Echo, Minnesota*.

But imitation is not innovation. Indeed, it demonstrates an actual lack of innovation. It may extend the life span of a real innovation—just as adding different styles can extend the lifespan of a genuine faucet innovation—but it does not add additional utility to the concept, and so it does not change anything fundamental.

Recyclers do have some value. Extending the life of an innovation is of economic value to the company. The danger comes when management confuses imitation with innovation and relies on imitation to continue growth. The person who comes up with *CSI: Echo, Minnesota* has extended the franchise for another year or two. The person who creates a new concept for Westerns to add to the TV lineup has created a new franchise. And new franchises are what innovation is all about. Sometimes less is enough. But the game winners offer something different and something to be aspired to.

You can have a building full of the right people, but you need to have something else as well: You need to have an organization that is designed to innovate and is managed so that it does so.

Chapter 11

Beating the Bureaucrats

So, WE HAVE COME A LONG WAY. WE HAVE WORKED THROUGH the three steps, and now we have a method that can lead us to product innovations. We have looked at staffing, and we have seen the differences between the types of people we need for *small* innovation and the types we need for *big* innovation. This gets us quite a distance down the road to innovative excellence. But it does not get us all the way there.

In the real world, it is not enough to have the right approach and the right people. To maximize innovation, that approach and those people must operate within an organization that fosters their task rather than merely tolerating it or actually inhibiting it. Excellence in method, in people, and in organization will yield excellence in innovation—and nothing less than excellence in all three areas will yield satisfactory results.

Creating a Culture of Innovation

As discussed earlier, one of the most powerful ways to achieve an innovating organization is to create a culture of innovation and to nourish that culture. And that is, on paper, a great approach. But culture is powerful. Even the strongest personalities bow to it to some degree. If the culture favors the status quo, if the culture is driven to make the trains run on time (not to create monorails that will be faster), then that is what will triumph. If the culture favors innovation, though, then innovation becomes possible. But how does that happen? How do you change something as powerful as culture?

There are three possibilities:

1. *Reward innovation.* All organizations think that they reward innovation. But do they really? Very often what starts out as a reward for innovation turns into an award for performance. Let me borrow from a previous career, in which I was focused on sentencing criminals. We know that potential criminals are deterred by potential punishment only if they think the punishment is highly certain, likely to be immediate, and greater than they think they can absorb. The flip side of these factors for reward would be highly certain, immediate, and generous. Of course, in both sentencing and rewarding, it is vital that you punish or reward the right person.

Let us look at each of the factors a little more closely:

A. *Highly certain.*—If you are going to motivate people to go one way or the other, they need to be pretty sure that the reward or punishment actually will follow from the approved-of or disapproved-of behavior. To the degree that they are unsure, they are unmotivated. In practice, this means that the reward process needs to be legitimate and transparent. If it is a backroom process run by a group of people who do not actually understand the product, it will be seen as a black box producing random results. If it is an open process with some level of peer input, it will gain credibility and stature.

B. *Immediate.* Picture this situation. An employee wants to push a couple of ideas. Both ideas are pretty good. But one of the ideas looks like a sure thing, while the other carries some risk with it. The two ideas would cost about the same to develop, but the riskier idea, if it works, will yield much greater results. Then add this to the equation: The reward program is not available until a product has been released and is successful. Which idea do you think the employee is motivated to pitch? The less risky one, of course, because that is what is rewarded and because management is announcing loudly that it is okay if you take a risk, but do not expect it to be there unless the project actually succeeds. For the reward to have meaning, it should come when the project is approved. Otherwise it simply provides an incentive for risk-free proposals.

C. *Generous.* Reward, like punishment, has to mean something. It has to express the value that management puts on the innovation. The bigger and more expensive the innovation, the greater the reward should be. One size fits all is fine for baseball caps, but demoralizing for people.

D. *The right people.* Implementation and innovation are two different things. In most, but not all, circumstances, implementation is the daily work of the great majority of employees. That an innovation is successfully implemented is assumed to be true. Ordinary implementation deserves no reward, just as small innovation deserves no reward. The fact that the implementation, though ordinary, takes place in the context of an extraordinary innovation does not make the implementation extraordinary. The coach who innovates a last-minute touchdown drive to win the Super Bowl deserves a reward. The guy who moves the yard markers does not. He just happened to be there doing his job. At the very least, this means keeping rewards for innovation and rewards for implementation separate. Extraordinary implementation should be rewarded, but it should be rewarded because *it* is extraordinary, not because it took place in the context of a great idea.

2. *Recruit innovators.* Well, we would all love to recruit innovators, but how do we know who they are? Is there a web site called www.recruitinnovators.com? No, there is not. I checked. But there are two methods that work: hiring people with a history of innovation, and hiring new people with the potential for innovation. The first is pretty straightforward but involves some risk. You are hiring someone who has innovated in one environment in the hope that she will continue to innovate in your environment. You can see what this person has actually done in the past, and that is a good basis for focusing on her. But, as they say in the mutual fund business, "Past performance is no guarantee of future results." And, you will probably pay a pretty penny for your risk when you hire an experienced innovator. The risks are not trivial. People stop innovating because they lose their creative spark through age or illness or other factors. People

have a spark in one area but not in another. People get lucky or are synergistically creative with another person. You cannot tell from a résumé. So hiring experienced innovators is no guarantee of success. Hiring recent graduates also has its risks, but the stakes are typically lower in terms of salary.

The question remains, though, how do you select for innovation? While I do not think there is a foolproof method, there are some criteria that can be very helpful. People who use both sides of the brain are favored possibilities. That is, candidates who show artistic talent (in any art) along with analytical talent are likely to possess the right attributes. One is not much good without the other in business because the creative side must be focused on commercial ends. This is the attribute of pragmatism discussed in Chapter 10. A surrogate for artistic talent is a multiplicity of interests. Such a person is inherently curious. Curiosity is closely related to two other skills mentioned in Chapter 10: observation and questioning. Thus, the curious person is very likely to be innovative as well. I would also look for passion. People who get excited about their ideas bring a strong tool for overcoming institutional barriers to innovation. If you can find an artistic person who has also obtained a degree in an analytical field (business, law, or engineering, for example), then you may have the complete package.

Just as it is crucial to have innovative people, it is important to have them as part of a diverse group. A group of 10 people who are individually great innovators, but who all think the same way will not come up with a range of innovations. A group of people with different backgrounds— different experiences in the industry, experience in different industries, different educations, different cultural origins—will see the same problem in different ways. Those different perspectives will lead to different solutions. Having a variety of solutions to the same problem will dramatically increase the odds of genuine innovation.

3. *Demand innovation.* This sounds stern and possibly even counterproductive, but I believe that setting expectations high is a key management tool. If we tell our managers and employees that we *expect* them to innovate, that we *expect* them to create new products and processes, and that we will *not accept* mere mutations or product line extensions as innovation, and if we repeat that message and reinforce it with incentives, we will see results. If, instead, we treat innovation as a kind of pleasant surprise, then we will be infrequently surprised. This aspect has a second advantage: If you demand innovation and set very high standards, you may not have to look for the innovators anymore. The good ones will come looking for you. Of course, their less talented colleagues who think they are great innovators will be knocking on your door as well. But at least you will not have to put out an ad and weed through 80 résumés.

Managing Innovators

Innovators can be difficult to manage. Their virtue is that they do not want to do things the way they have always been done, and that can be an issue in hierarchical management situations. Innovators can be eccentric, temperamental, and even arrogant. Of course, the same descriptions would fit more than a few noninnovators as well, and corporations do seem to find ways to deal with the arrogant noninnovator.

There are several things that are useful in managing innovators:

- *Innovators should be managed by innovators.* Innovators tend to respect people based on their level of innovative ability. In particular, most innovators have more ideas than they have good ideas. Yet they bridle when someone rejects their latest brainstorm. If they perceive the person who is rejecting the idea as an innovator, then they will not go off thinking that the manager "just doesn't get it." They might even accept the possibility that they had missed something important and reevaluate their proposal.

- *Innovators feed off one another.* Innovators need to rub elbows with one another, exchange ideas, and be energized by other passionate and off-center thinkers. They compete with one another, and they add fresh insight to one another's work. This need is hard to meet in a large organization. The units are spread out geographically, and even when they are in one location, it is hard to get a handle on who is doing what, to say nothing of who is doing what well. But this problem can be dealt with in two ways. The first is to create an innovation consultants group, a kind of SWAT team that moves from area to area. This would also help to deal with staleness, which is discussed in the next paragraph. A second approach is to form and foster a peer group to which several different areas would nominate their best innovator; the group would then meet on a regular basis to share ideas and gain feedback. Communication among innovators will yield more innovation, and so any reasonable method of enhancing that communication would be useful.

* *Innovators can grow stale.* They need regular rotation, moving into entirely new areas, to refresh their batteries and get the creative juices flowing again (to mix at least two metaphors). Three years is a long time for an innovator to be focused on one area. Moving the innovator may cause short-term issues for the former focus area, but the long-term effects of rotation outweigh these, in my mind. If we began to think of innovators as a shared resource, rotation would be much more acceptable.

The last two points quickly merge into the idea of internal innovation consultants. Many companies have used external innovation consultants successfully. These people have the great value of being able to see methodology and organizational issues that are hard for people on the inside to see clearly. But they have absolutely no knowledge of your customers or your products, and six weeks after they first show up, they are gone, leaving only an invoice behind. They can point out what you are doing wrong, and that service is enormously valuable. But doing things right is your task, and it starts with people who understand your customers, your industry, and your product.

Internal innovation consultants have the knowledge and the aptitude that you need. When those attributes are coupled with the broader methodological knowledge of the outside consultants, the combination is very powerful. Once the internal and external consultants have worked out the appropriate method and begun to institute it, the internal consultants are all that the business needs.

This brings up another central point in organizing for innovation.

Who Owns Product Innovation?

The easy answer is to say that everyone does. It is also the wrong answer. No one would ever say, "Everyone owns finance" or, "Everyone owns marketing." No one owns a task that everyone owns.

For a quarter century, George MacKinnon sat on the U.S. Court of Appeals in Washington. Before that, he had been a member of Congress and had held a variety of other important positions. But he was probably proudest of having played football for the University of Minnesota. Indeed, even in his eighties he looked like he could still play the game. He had many stories, but this one is very appropriate:

In the mid-1920s, the University of Minnesota had lost a crucial game because it had allowed its opponent to run back a kickoff for a touchdown. On Monday at practice, the coach did not mention the failure. Instead, he told eleven players to run back a kick and two players to defend against the runback. Surprisingly, the two defenders made the tackle. The coach told them to repeat the effort. Again they made the tackle. Then the coach called the team over and said, "Last Saturday, eleven of you could not stop the runback. Today, two of you could. The difference is that when there were eleven of you, no one thought it was *their* job. When there were only two of you, you knew it was *your* job."

That is a powerful story. It points out graphically what we all know intuitively: Unless someone is accountable for getting things done, things will not get done. Committees will not do it. Task forces will not do it. Aphorisms ("We are all responsible for _____") will not do it. Only an accountable and empowered manager can get things done.

So how does this apply to innovation? The problem is that innovation does not have a natural home in some companies. In a company that produces technology products, innovation may be seen as a technology function. In a consumer products company, innovation may be seen as a marketing function. In a pharmaceutical company, innovation it may be a function of some combination of doctors and biochemists. And each of these variations may make sense in the context in which it is found. But in most companies, the situation is squishy. There may be a new product development group, and that may be in marketing or technology or it may be stand-alone.

In the end, these structural issues probably do not matter. If all large organizations are matrixed, then the location of innovation is merely another spot on the matrix. What is important with regard to its location is that management understands that each location has a bias and understands the nature of that bias. If innovation is seen as a Technology function, then the concepts it produces are likely to be products that are reasonable from a technology perspective. That may mean they are the products that best match the company's existing technological competencies or that use the most interesting new technology. Those attributes may or may not coincide with customer needs. It may be easier to program a feature in Java, and so, from a technology perspective, it may be a no-brainer to do the project in Java. But if Java runs slower in this particular usage, then it is the customer who pays the price for the gain in programming efficiency.

If, on the other hand, innovation is in Marketing, its decisions may reflect a bias toward products that appear to present powerful marketing opportunities. A given product may be able to be marketed as "energy efficient" and thus attract market share from those potential customers who are concerned about global warming. But this marketing advantage may be short-lived and may lead the company to pass on a product innovation with a longer shelf life.

There is nothing wrong with either Technology or Marketing or Manufacturing having a role in product innovation, so long as it is absolutely clear which manager is responsible for achieving the goals. It is that person's task to take the biases into account, to balance them against each other, and to create a pipeline of product innovations that make sense to customers in spite of those biases and in spite of the fact that the manager is forced to operate in a matrixed environment. What matters in the end is clear accountability. Without that, the job will simply not get done, and there will be no one to blame for the failure. That's a disaster scenario in which everyone signs off on a project but no one is responsible for the results of that project. No business can afford that kind of approach.

Summing things up, innovation will be important if management thinks it is important and adequately conveys that message to employees through communications, organization, and incentives. Innovation will follow if the company is staffed and managed for innovation and is expected to innovate. Otherwise, innovation will simply be random. It may happen, or it may not happen. That is not good enough, because if a company is to grow, innovation *must* happen. It is too important to leave to chance.

In the next chapter, we will move away from innovation itself and take a look at how the approach we have discussed can help top management decide what it should fund and what it should not fund, and how these same questions can help guide other aspects of the organization.

Chapter 12

Straightening Out the Rest of the Company

MOST OF WHAT HAS BEEN SAID SO FAR IS DIRECTED AT THE product development staff. The questions posed provide such people with an approach to looking at products that is strongly customer-focused, pragmatic, and easy to implement. When used in this way, they are a tool for ideation— for the creation and prioritization of new product concepts. They also serve as a template for designing the products that emerge from this ideation. Using these questions, the product development staff should be able to come forward with, test, and refine new product concepts.

But that is not the end of the process of product innovation because the good folks in Product Development are not the only people who pass on a product idea, nor are they the only ones who play a role in its implementation. Products are approved through a business case process that is likely to involve Finance, Sales, and Marketing and may involve the CEO and the CFO as well.

Products are built by Manufacturing or Technology according to user requirements and specifications drawn up in a cooperative process with Product Development. Such processes involve give and take—change—in the product definition. And they also involve some decisions that the entity building the product makes in isolation from Product Development.

Products are brought to market by Sales and Marketing, and in so doing they position the product to the customer in ways that are intended to make it simple for the customer to grasp the value proposition. This positioning depends entirely on these departments' view of the product and their view of the customer. That may or may not coincide with the ideas that were in the mind of Product Development.

The questions can play an important role in each of these additional tasks. Just as importantly, they can help align the various groups working on the product around a common mission by giving them a common understanding. Decisions about the details of manufacturing a product and decisions about positioning it are based in part on an image of what the product will be used for—what tasks the user values. The better aligned all parts of the company are as to what those tasks are, the more likely it is that the product and its presentation to the customer will be focused and on target.

Let us look more closely at each of the corporate areas involved.

Business Case Approval

There is a lot of expense involved in bringing out a new product.

There is the cost of creating the product itself, and that can be considerable. A product needs to have specifications. A plan to build it by implementing those specifications must be created. Materials must be gathered. Machinery must be adjusted or created. Quality standards need to be established and implemented. Workers must be paid. With technology products, programmers may have to be hired, and new servers and other hardware may need to be obtained.

But that is just the beginning. Any new product requires packaging, training for customer support, implementation of accounting activities, education of the sales force, creation of marketing and sales collateral materials, booking of advertising space, piloting, and a whole host of other activities that bring the product from the minds and drawing boards of its creators to the hands of customers. New product launches are the engines of growth, and these engines need a lot of fuel. The fuel in this case is money. And money is not handed out just because someone in Product Development thinks he has a hot idea.

Any significant product launch is going to require approval up the food chain. A business case will need to be prepared; this case will have to demonstrate to upper management that the product can be built at a certain cost and marketed in a certain way, and it will estimate the number of units that can be sold. When presented to these final arbiters, the business case will appear totally reasonable, and the arithmetic will all be done correctly (or, at least, it will be done in such a way that hurdle rates are met). But, as anyone who has ever participated in this process knows, that business case will be built on a set of assumptions, and that is where the problem lies.

There is nothing in the world that is easier than reasoning perfectly from a set of false assumptions. And false assumptions are not always detected. If you can put a smokescreen over your assumptions, or if they go unchallenged, or if they just happen to be wrong, the rest is easy. Let us look at an example.

In Chapter 5 there was an example of a device to help hang pictures. The device reduced the number of steps need to hang a picture from 20 down to 10. That is, on its face, a great thing. We can imagine the presentation to upper management.

The PowerPoint show would begin with an estimate of market size. There would be an estimate of the number of pictures sold every year and presumably hung on walls. There would then be an estimate of the amount of money spent on picture-hanging tools each year. The next slide would demonstrate the complexity of the picture-hanging task and show how long it takes to actually hang a picture. A further slide would announce that a breakthrough had been made, that millions of units could be sold at a price of $29.95 apiece, and that the margins would be in excess of 40 percent. A return on invested capital (or whatever other metric is fashionable that year) would be calculated, and the result of that calculation would be highly satisfactory.

Then the prototype device would be pulled out from under a table. A picture (presumably a flattering portrait of the CEO) would be brought in, and the same CEO would be asked to designate a spot for hanging the picture. One . . . two . . . three: The device would be used, the picture hung, and the business case approved. High fives to be exchanged later at a local watering hole.

Not so fast.

There is a hidden assumption in here, and that assumption is absolutely crucial to the success of this product. The assumption is that customers will grasp the value of the device immediately and therefore will be willing to invest money to buy it and time to learn how to use it.

But our picture-hanging device, while clever, may not be really intuitive. It may appear to customers to be some weird Rube Goldberg machine instead. There is a legitimate question as to whether someone wandering down the aisles of Home Depot would look at it and say, "Wow! There it is! The answer to all my picture-hanging woes!" or would say instead, "What the heck is that thing?" The device may be easy to use, but is it easy to learn to use?

This takes us back to the net utility issue we have discussed before, and that issue was not a part of the PowerPoint presentation. The device looked easy to use because the person demonstrating the prototype was an expert at using it. She had helped design it to begin with, and she had spent an hour practicing for this demonstration. Think of those magical food-processing devices on the infomercials. You can do anything in almost no time with perfect results every single time—if you are the person doing the infomercial and you have practiced your routine for two weeks and can refilm a segment when you make a mistake. But the average user who orders the device may give up even before he gets the thing assembled.

It would not take much effort to find out about the net utility issue. Take the same prototype and try it out with some real customers. You would not even need to spend any money on doing so. Everyone hangs pictures, so grab five people from Finance and HR and ask them to try it out while you watch. But unless someone asks about net utility, that may well not happen. The presenter may well evade the point because a product developer who is presenting a product tends to stay away from the weak points and emphasize the sizzle factors.

So the product may get approved just because the numbers looked good and no one had enough information to challenge the assumption.

Now, let us look at this presentation from a different perspective. Let us imagine a meeting in which the presenter is required to demonstrate that the questions described in this book have been used and that the overriding concept of net utility has been applied. Now we have a very different meeting and, perhaps, a different outcome.

First of all, the presenter must adequately describe the task that the customer is really engaged in. That task is not "putting a nail into a wall." Nor is it "measuring the space between two walls, finding the center point, and putting a pencil mark there." The task is "hanging a picture."

Second, the presenter must show *in detail* how the task is carried out now. She must lay out the specific steps that the customer presently engages in to complete the task. Then she must show the steps involved in the innovation. Finally, she must demonstrate that the innovation actually yields net utility when compared to the old method, taking into account the required learning.

Suddenly we are not talking about a slick PowerPoint show anymore. Now the fact that the CEO and CFO may be further removed from direct market contact than they would like is no longer relevant. Because now the product presenter is forced to explain in detail what the customer experience is and then explain in detail how the innovation enhances that experience. There is not a lot of room for blue smoke and mirrors in this scenario. At the end, the executives reviewing the proposal will know whether the product people have really understood the customer experience and will know if they have really proposed something that will notably improve that experience.

Of course, the concept of net utility will always retain a certain degree of subjectivity that may not be fully resolved in the presentation. All of us will measure this differently. The infamous early adopters will always be optimistic about the gain they will get from a new product. Cynics will always be pessimistic. But if the issues surrounding a product can be reduced to a narrow question of net utility, a bit of the observational market research described in Chapter 3 should resolve the problem.

This is a somewhat unhappy picture for the Product Development folks. Showmanship will not be enough. They actually will have to explain to the CFO, who has never seen a live customer, how that customer thinks and what he does and how he will react to this new notion, and the CFO is going to have the tools to question their statements. People in green eyeshades armed with knowledge present a formidable barrier to product approval.

But there is a bright side as well. If the right approach has been used in the development of the product proposal, the answers to the questions are already available and validated. Moreover, these answers will most often be derived from the first two questions. However, the product developer can use the product approval process to tease out the prospects raised by Step 3, achieving workflow integration. This can set the stage and ease the path for the next level of product proposals.

Building the Product

A product is nothing until it is built. The people who design a product and the people who build a product are rarely the same. These two groups have to communicate clearly with each other to get the job done, and communication, especially on an innovative product, can be quite difficult. Recall the scene described in the introduction to Part 1 where the Italian courts were planning to implement a dramatic innovation in criminal procedure. We floundered because we could not communicate with each other, and we could not communicate with each other because the question was new and we had no pattern for bridging the cultural gap between us. That problem is endemic in innovation.

Let us look at an example using our picture-hanging device.

An integral part of the device is the telescoping rods that help us to center the picture between two points. There are two ways to produce this feature. One is to have a handle in the center that turns a gear. That gear then moves the two rods out by equal amounts with each turn, so that they are always the same length and thus the handle is always at the center. A second way to achieve this is to have markers on each rod so that you can move one out to 4'7" and then do the same with the other. This second approach would be significantly easier and cheaper to build and would present fewer quality and maintenance issues—but it would add steps to the process, and steps are what we are trying to eliminate. Without input from Product Development, Manufacturing might proceed on the assumption that the second choice was better because *from a manufacturing perspective,* it is better. It is easier and cheaper to make, and it probably will present fewer quality problems. Even if Manufacturing does not go off on its own but consults with Product Development, that process means there will be some delay in getting to market, and delay always equals expense.

If the user requirements are not explicitly used to make the choice, then the product may end up being inferior to the concept. If, on the other hand, Manufacturing is taken through the process that led to the product concept, then the likelihood of confusion is significantly reduced. In addition, if the people in the manufacturing group fully understand the purposes of the innovation, they may well suggest improvements themselves as they confront the challenge of building the product. That can only help to make better products.

Sales and Marketing

No product can succeed unless it is properly presented to the appropriate customers. To do that, Sales and Marketing need to fully understand the product and, in particular, what the product means to the end customer. What exactly is the value proposition for this innovation? What types of people will want to use it? Why will they want to use it? What difference will it make in their lives? How much will they gain from the use of it?

These questions are all vital to positioning the product. They lead to a list of benefits that will be emphasized. They help in creating the marketing theme. They help in designing the packaging. They help in setting the pricing. They help in determining the target audience. And, to a substantial degree, the answers to these questions can be found in the answers to the questions that have already been asked during ideation.

If we fully understand the real task that people are engaged in, and if we have significantly reduced the steps needed to carry out that task, then we have advanced the position dramatically because we have understood the customer and the customer has defined the positioning for us. Because we have understood the customers' task and observed it before and after our innovation, we know with considerable accuracy exactly who those customers are and what they are gaining from this advance. We know what it is that they find useful and valuable about the product.

Because we have had intense customer contact and we have solved problems for our customers that they may not even be consciously aware that they have, we can take their actual reactions and form marketing approaches around them. Because we can often literally see the moment when the customer recognizes the gain in net utility, we can use that "Aha!" moment to make the sale.

Again, let us use the picture hanger as an example. The product has been designed. It has been manufactured. Now Sales and Marketing move to the fore. What have they got? Well, they have a device that helps you to hang pictures. That's good. It looks a little complicated to use. That's bad. It's a little unwieldy in size. That may make it harder to get shelf space in Home Depot. That's *really* bad.

Suddenly Sales and Marketing are starting to wonder if they have a stinker on their hands. Some wag starts referring to it as Project Edsel or New Coke. The risk of self-fulfilling prophecy is becoming serious, and that could absolutely kill this product before it even gets out the door.

But exposure to the analysis derived from the ideation process can change all that. The product has some complications to it, yes, but it is much less complicated than the traditional method. So the approach may be to show how hard it is to hang pictures now and then promise greater simplicity.

The product is large for shelf items in the hardware section at Home Depot. But the product is not designed for handymen and do-it-yourselfers. It is designed for people who do not like the challenge of hanging a picture properly, people who have seriously thought about hiring somebody to hang pictures for them. So maybe it does not belong at Home Depot. Maybe it belongs in the picture frame section at department stores and in picture-framing shops. And maybe a higher price point can be attached to it in those places because it is in a fancier locale than the nuts and bolts aisle at your local hardware store.

Instead of despair in Sales and Marketing, we have the excitement of a new opportunity with high customer value, and perhaps even a new channel for distributing our products. The problem has not changed. The market must still be convinced that the product provides a strong net utility, but instead of despair, we have challenge and opportunity. That is a very big difference.

Of course, it is perfectly true that many companies in fact are not thrilled by the possibility of challenge and change. Change represents risk, and those in commodity businesses (and their less forgivable counterparts in growth businesses who think like those in commodity businesses) are risk averse. Their expertise is in market share angles and cost cutting, not in new paradigms. They do remember New Coke.

Proper application of this approach should buck up even these fainthearted souls. When you have a product that clearly improves the customer experience, and when the product development process, business case process, and manufacturing or development processes are all lined up behind it, Sales and Marketing will get behind it as well, even in a commodity business.

So, while the core users of this method will always be the people in Product Development, the questions can also be used as a means of aligning the matrixed parts toward a single goal with a common understanding of the purposes behind the project. Instead of diffused efforts and mismatched goals, this approach provides intense organizational focus. It can be used, as well, as an effective filter during the product approval process and as a way of using that process to ensure that all product activities are centered on customers.

Sample Answers to Innovation Workout 3

A. *Going to the Movies.* A couple is in line to buy tickets at your movie theater. They get to the cash register and order two tickets for *The Monster that Devoured Cleveland,* and then you warmly surprise them by . . . ?????

You surprise them by taking their food orders and collecting the money at the same time as they buy their tickets. The food order is transmitted to a counter, where it is ready for them when they are through buying the tickets. One person handles sodas, another handles popcorn, and another handles everything else. There are no wasted steps and no making change. There is one less cash transaction and one less line to wait in. If the movie line is long, a customer could fill in a machine-readable form that would simultaneously add the cost of the food to his movie bill and send his order along to the concession stand to be filled. Or food could be sold in special bundles with the ticket. If the standard food order is a medium popcorn and a medium soda for $7.50, why not sell a ticket that includes that bundle for $7 extra? Then the customer takes a coupon to a special counter and gets handed a medium popcorn and a medium soda cup, which she then fills herself.

Oh, and while they are at it, they could pay the parking fee at the same time.

B. *Parking the car.* You own an airport long-term parking concession. It is typically crowded, and customers typically do not return for three days. A customer comes to your lot, pushes the button on the ticket machine, and is delighted to learn . . . ?????

You surprise your customers by giving them an assigned parking spot automatically. They do not have to spend any time looking for a spot. Instead, they just drive directly to it—*and* when they come back, their parking ticket has their space location on it, so they do not have to wander around repeating the infamous *Seinfeld* episode. A simpler alternative is to have the machine assign the customer to a floor where it knows that parking spaces are available. The ticket would be coded to allow the customer access to that floor.

C. *Caller ID.* The phone rings at home, and your caller ID system tells you that your son, who has just moved, is calling from his new number. You are very pleased with your caller ID provider because . . . ?????

Your provider has placed a handy screen that says "Replace Old Number with New Number?" You click a button and your address book is updated without your having to do contortionist tricks with your thumbs on the tiny keyboard.

D. *Responding to E-Mail.* An e-mail arrives from someone you have not previously received e-mail from. You read it and respond to it. Your e-mail program takes things one step further by . . . ?????

Your program jumps to the next step and includes the person in your address book. Your responding to her validates your interest in her. For the persnickety, an "Include in Address Book?" dialog box could come up to confirm your approval.

More Innovation Workouts

Adults learn by doing. You can read this book five times and have the process down pat, but this would not be as valuable as reading it once and completing all of the workouts, and also making up some of your own. You will very quickly find that the approach you take in completing these workouts becomes instinctive. You will find yourself relying less and less on memorized rules and more and more on learned behavior. At some point, you may start annoying other people by constantly pointing out innovation opportunities. Then you will know you really have it down pat.

For these workouts, an innovation opportunity will be described on one page and a sample answer will be shown on the next. Again, the answers are not the "right" ones; they are a means for you to validate your own answers. Avoid

"Superman" answers in which some magic, but as yet unknown, piece of technology solves the problem by spinning the Earth backward and turning back time. Every answer should involve simple applications of well-known methods—things that can be implemented starting tomorrow without either divine intervention or a Nobel Prize–winning breakthrough.

These workouts can also form the basis of a team development program. There is something about competing that brings out the best in each of us, and competing on workouts such as these will sharpen your group skills as well as help management to identify which employees show the most consistent innovative strength.

You may also find it extremely useful to start developing your own workouts. Here is why. This book has emphasized a method for innovating in whatever product field you work in. But the method of innovation does not necessarily tell you where all the opportunities for innovation are. If you follow this approach, you will find many opportunities, but you probably will not find them all. To do that, your eye and your mind must become trained to look for opportunities everywhere, and developing workouts such as these can help to do that.

For instance, you may find yourself on a cold Wisconsin day trying to find a parking space in a crowded mall parking lot and having space after space blocked by abandoned shopping carts, as in the first of these workouts.

The Case of the Abandoned Shopping Carts

In a last-ditch effort to disprove the concept of global warming, a cold wind has come across the Arctic icecap, crossed western Canada, and roared straight down into the heart of Wisconsin. A lone shopper pulls into a parking lot at a local mall. Hearty Wisconsinites have filled nearly all the available spaces, despite the fact that the temperature is in the minus zone. Our shopper spies a space and goes to swoop into it, only to discover that it is blocked by two abandoned shopping carts. There is a corral for such carts a few spaces down, but there is not much upside to parking the car in the lane, getting out and moving the carts, and then pulling into the space. The problem cannot be "solved," but it can be prevented. All you have to do is think up a way to do that. Remember that here your customer is actually the store—the owner of the shopping carts, the outfit that has to either hire more employees to round up the carts or lose customers who do not want to park in Siberia in midwinter.

Sample Answer for the Shopping Cart Problem

We start with a slight variation on Step 1. The "product" here is actually a service, and the real service is the efficient provision of shopping carts so that they are easy to obtain and use and do not present problems to customers, such as blocking parking spaces.

The steps as currently structured are:

1. Obtain a shopping cart.
2. Use it for shopping.
3. Use it to take your goods to your car.
4. Abandon it (especially when it is cold).
5. Have a store employee eventually round it up along with others.
6. Have the employee return the collected carts to the front of the store.

What we want to do here is to eliminate as much as we can of Steps 4 through 6. We can achieve that by focusing on Step 4. Step 4 is crucial because if the carts are not abandoned, but instead are placed in a corral or, even better, returned to the front of the store, then Step 5 and possibly Step 6 disappear as well. The carts do not need to be rounded up because the customers have already done that, and possibly they do not need to be brought to the front of the store for the same reason.

So now we have a simple problem of incentives. How do

we give customers an incentive to behave differently? The answer is simple and traditional: money.

Many European businesses have already solved the problem. The shopping carts are nested just as in American stores, but each cart is connected to the one in front by a chain with a probe on the front that connects from the handle of one cart to the handle of the one in front. If you want a cart, you must release the probe by putting a coin worth roughly 60 to 80 cents in a slot. As the probe is released, the coin is locked in. When the probe is reinserted after you return the cart to a cart station, the coin is released.

There are two objections to this approach:

1. It is inconvenient to have to have the right coin.
2. The incentive is too low to be of use in America on a cold day.

As to the first concern, in Europe stores sell and automobile dealers provide on their key chains a disc that fits in instead. As long as there is a cost in time and money for replacing the disc, people will use and retain it.

As to the second, assume that two quarters are required. For every 10 shoppers who abandon their 50 cents, there will be one teenager interested in making a quick 5 bucks.

This is one form of incentive or disincentive to eliminate these steps. Can you think of others? Can you think of an entirely different approach?

Making the Bed

Sheets have been used for centuries, but there have been very few advances in the product itself. There have been different styles and different fabrics, and there have been "wrinkle-free" models, but there has been only one real innovation: the elastic-cornered bottom sheet that has made that piece of bedding somewhat easier to install.[1]

So sheets are about as much of a commodity product as bread once was—before the invention of the slicer. Your challenge is to break that commodity cycle.

Sample Answer for the Bed-Making Problem

As always, we start by looking at the steps (one verb = one step) involved in making the bed. Here we focus only on the sheet portion.

1. Get the sheets from storage.
2. Select the bottom sheet.
3. Spread the bottom sheet on the bed.
4. Position the elastic corners under the mattress.
5. Get the top sheet.
6. Find the hem that belongs at the head of the bed.
7. Position the sheet so that the hem is facing correctly.
8. Spread the top sheet on the bed.
9. Align it so that it is even on both sides and the bottom has enough cloth to tuck in.
10. Tuck the top sheet under the mattress at the foot.
11. Smooth the sheet.

One quick look at this list shows us that our problem is with putting on the top sheet. Doing this takes seven steps, whereas putting on the actually more complex bottom sheet takes three. And look closely at Steps 6 through 10. Those steps take up most of the labor, and they seem to be inefficient. Think back to our picture-hanging device. The steps here of finding the right hem, aligning it on the bed, and so forth seem quite reminiscent of that activity. Is all that activity really necessary? I think not.

What if the two sheets were a single unit? What if the

top sheet was permanently sewed to the bottom sheet or was easily fastened to it by snaps (Velcro will not work—you can figure out why)? Then Steps 5, 6, 7, 9, and 10 would go away, and Step 8 would be simplified. Indeed, maybe the bottom sheet could be altered as well so that it snapped to the bottom of the mattress and the whole elastic thing could be eliminated, making it easier to fold the sheets for storage.

Will this plan save time and effort? That would be easy to determine. A prototype could be built for less than $50 (counting the sheets and the labor). Then you can run a few experiments and have a very good sense of whether you have net utility—that is, whether you have a product or not.

The Dry-Cleaning Problem

This problem will be a little bit different and a bit more challenging as well. Here you will need to reinvent an industry. Fear not. You are near the end of the book, so you must be up to the challenge.

As noted, most of this book is focused on product development. But, as we saw in Chapter 8, the lessons of this book frequently apply to services as well. Dry cleaning is a very common service. There are 30,000 dry-cleaning companies in the United States—one for every 10,000 people. Even in small towns there will be one or more dry-cleaning operations. The industry is very fragmented, with the 50 largest companies controlling less than half of the market share. This is a people-driven service, with the average revenue per employee being $60,000.[2]

Yet the industry is caught in the TV version of the 1950s. June Cleaver is free all day, except for the occasional bridge club. She takes the dry cleaning to the neighborhood shop, where everyone knows her, some morning when she is not baking brownies, and then, a week later, she picks it up between catching Eddie Haskell in his latest stunt and cooking Ward's dinner.

If that world ever existed, it does not exist any more. June is working 10-hour days, and she and Ward are taking the kids to soccer games on Saturday. So the dry cleaner should be open later to accommodate them or have locations that are more convenient for them. But it can't do that. Its labor costs are destroying its margins already, and staying open another 10 to 12 hours per week will not be possible. Real estate is its next highest expense, and it cannot afford to open mini-locations on the same revenue base. What to do?

As discussed earlier, the questions we have gone through are framed somewhat differently in the services world. The emphasis in the labor-intensive services world will always be on taking out the labor because that is where the cost and the management wear and tear are. But to do that, you need to focus on what the people do and ask yourself, "Is that a step that needs to be done and that needs to be done by a person?" You then have the choice of eliminating the step or automating it.

So, your task in this workout is to figure out a way to accommodate Ward and June's frantic schedule, given the dry-cleaning industry's need to control labor costs and minimize real estate expenses.

Sample Answer to the Dry Cleaning Problem

This problem, being a services problem, requires a slightly different approach. We know what the task is. For Ward and June, the task is getting their dry cleaning done. We know that they are unhappy with the inconvenience of the current situation and will reward any dry cleaner who improves it for them. For the dry cleaner, we know that the innovation that solves Ward and June's problem cannot add greatly to costs.

There are three general strategies that could be looked at here. First, the dry cleaner could increase its hours and thus add staff if the owner could find some offsetting expense savings. We know that if we wrote out all the steps involved in dry cleaning, we might find some offsetting ways to save costs, but for the moment we will assume that the dry cleaner is operating efficiently.

Second, the dry cleaner could outsource the collection of dry cleaning at rates lower than those currently paid to employees. That is, the dry cleaner could find local businesses, such as convenience stores, that are open extended hours and could contract with those businesses to receive and deliver dry cleaning. There would be some additional cost. The dry cleaner would have to pay fees to the convenience store or other business, and a truck would have to make regular pickups. But this is a real potential solution, especially assuming that it would lead to a noticeable growth in revenue, offsetting the new costs. This approach is a variation on Step 3. It asks, "If I cannot efficiently complete the customer's task because I cannot stay open extended hours, what other service that my customer uses does stay open longer hours?" The answer might be a convenience store or a service station, and a deal might be made with such a business to accept dry cleaning.

Third, the dry cleaner could automate. Collection boxes could be set up at various locales with video recording of transactions. Again, the dry cleaner would have to pay someone to pick up the dry cleaning, and, absent a black box technology involving a coded way to pick up dry cleaning at an unattended kiosk, this solves only half the problem—the dropping off of dry cleaning. But it does so at a low price in a one-time cost. Automation is simply a form of Step 2. It takes steps out of the process by automating them.

So, of the three strategies, at least two show some promise deserving further exploration. The third involves a top to bottom review of the efficiency of the business, and, while that is beyond our scope, it is nonetheless worth pursuing in the real world.

The Buying a Car Problem

Another service problem will be useful. This area is particularly complex and ripe for innovation, so developing our innovation muscles here will be very useful.

We all buy cars. Some of us buy many cars. Some of us buy cars frequently. But most adults will buy several cars in their lifetime. The transaction is very similar to that of buying a house: It is multistaged, it involves several service providers, and it is inefficient. It can also be annoying in many ways, particularly during the negotiation process. For this example, however, we will assume that we have a modern car dealer who has a fixed price that is reasonable and that we have chosen a car and are prepared to buy it.

Here are the steps that were involved the last time I did this:

1. I picked out a car.
2. I waited 30 minutes to meet with the financing person.
3. She asked me a series of questions about my income and employment and so forth and entered the answers into a program on her computer. This took another 15 minutes of my time and 15 minutes of her time.
4. The computer qualified me.
5. She printed out the paperwork, and I reviewed and signed it. Another 15 minutes.
6. I was told that the car would be "prepped" and would be ready for pickup the next day.

7. I went home, called my insurer, and obtained insurance on the car.
8. I returned the next day and picked up the car with temporary plates.
9. I filled out the paperwork for permanent plates and mailed it in.
10. The plates arrived 10 days later.
11. I put on the permanent plates.

That is the problem. Needing 11 steps for this transaction is bad enough. But needing 11 steps involving a lot of waiting and going back and forth to the dealer is ridiculous.

So, make my life easier and make a fortune for yourself by solving this problem.

Sample Solution to the Buying a Car Problem

This is a very nice problem because it gives us good possibilities to work with on both Step 1 and Step 2. Let us take a look at the steps we listed:

1. I picked out a car.
2. I waited 30 minutes to meet with the financing person.
3. She asked me a series of questions about income and employment and so forth and entered the answers into a program on her computer. This took another 15 minutes of my time and 15 minutes of her time.
4. The computer qualified me.
5. She printed out the paperwork, and I reviewed and signed it. Another 15 minutes.
6. I was told that the car would be "prepped" and would be ready for pickup the next day.
7. I went home, called my insurer, and obtained insurance on the car.
8. I returned the next day and picked up the car with temporary plates.
9. I filled out the paperwork for permanent plates and mailed it in.
10. The plates arrived 10 days later.
11. I put on the permanent plates.

First, let us see what steps we can make more efficient through combination or elimination. Look at items 2 through

5. Envision a situation in which, after I select a dealer, I go to its web site, enter the information myself, print out the paperwork, and bring it with me. An hour or more of my time has been saved, and about double the amount of their time.[3]

Now take a look at steps 7 and 9. All of the information needed for these tasks has been obtained in the course of financing the car. Both steps could easily be automated away. And if this was my first car and I did not already have automobile insurance, the same program that let me fill out the financing forms before I went to the dealer could have offered me a choice of insurance vendors and forwarded the information to them for quotes.

Next, with the time and money the dealer has saved through my filling out the forms, it could easily deliver the car to me.

Finally, what is with the temporary plates? Give the dealers a stock of plates with some security involved, and let them issue them and put them on during the "prep" process. If that is too scary, then the DMV should put its offices in those same strips of highway where the car dealers are and have a drive-in window where it hands out plates, thus reducing the inconvenience significantly.

Going to the Airport

I fly a lot and I hate doing so. In the good old days, (30 years ago) flying was a pleasure. Not so any more. Now we have friction point after friction point. Stress factor is added upon stress factor. The list of problems with flying is nearly endless. Yet there seems to be very little innovation in this area. Perhaps because the bureaucracies are so daunting.

Set forth below is a pretty ordinary set of the steps one takes when flying these days. Ignoring the fact that trying to change both the U.S. government policies and the practices of economically marginal airlines is a daunting one, see how many of these steps you can knock out, simplify, or combine. For this workout let's assume that you are willing to pay a reasonable amount extra to avoid some of the major hurdles. Be careful here. This is one where it is pretty easy to invent a Rube Goldberg solution. Simplicity is the best approach and Net Utility is a must. You do not want to add more complication to the agony of flying.

1. View schedule
2. Make reservation
3. Pack for trip
4. Put your toothpaste in a baggie and separate it from the rest of your luggage
5. Get luggage to the airport
6. Get yourself to the airport
7. Get boarding pass
8. Check in luggage (if necessary)
9. Get through security

10. Get luggage through security
11. Retrieve your luggage
12. Get to gate

One hint. This is a complex services situation. Your job is to seamlessly connect the dots.

Sample Answer for Going to the Airport

The trick here is to solve this in such a way as to avoid just replacing one old step with a new one. The goal is to offload as much of the work to one other entity as possible. In that way this workout is very similar to the real estate transaction discussion in the chapter on services. There, you always have to deal with a broker so the broker is the obvious place to offload the rest to. Here, the situation is a little more complex. But the answer stills needs to be simple in order to meet the Net Utility standard.

Many a business traveler gets to the airport via a car service. Those services are a bit expensive for many travelers, but would they still be too expensive if, for an additional price, they obtained your boarding pass, picked you up at home, dropped you off at a VIP security line, and checked your luggage for you? They might even arrange for your carry-on luggage to be delivered to you at your gate or for a tube of life-threatening toothpaste to be in your hotel room. Such a service could combine Steps 4–11 and that would make my traveling, at least, much easier.

Is This Any Way to Run a Restaurant?

The next couple of workouts will take different approaches from the ones we have done so far.

This workout will not ask you to solve a problem with an innovation. Instead it will ask you to look at an innovation and ask if it makes sense. Recall that the 3 Steps are used not just to innovate but also to evaluate innovation efforts. They can help us to separate good innovative efforts from bad ones. This first workout will give you some sense of what that means in practice.

The next two workouts after this one will ask you to solve a problem but they will not describe the current methods and steps. Instead they will pose what I call a "clean desk" situation. That is, the problem will be presented to you as if no one had ever tackled it before. Instead of examining the current paradigm and deleting or combining steps, your task will be to pretend that you are the first person ever to consider this issue and to create an approach from scratch. Then you can critically examine your own steps as well as applying the principle of net utility. This approach can be helpful when it is particularly hard to break away from the existing model because we are so used to how it operates.

Now, let's visit a restaurant.

There are two chain restaurants that I am aware of that operate in an unusual way. One of these chains exists in Europe and North America. The other is confined to Europe.

Here is how they work: The customer enters the restaurant and is handed a slip of paper with various items listed (in one chain) or a kind of debit card (in the other). Then the customer goes to various stations spread around the restaurant. There may be a Pasta section, a Salad section, Entrees and so forth. At each station the customer tells the person what they want, gets the item and puts it on their tray and the employee marks the slip of paper or debits their card. Then the customer goes to a cash register and submits their slip or card and pays the bill. So, the format is very much like that of a cafeteria, but instead of having one serving line, it has several. And instead of having one register attendant who examines and prices the items selected, this model has each item priced at the station where it originated.

Sample Answer to the Restaurant Problem

Two questions come to mind each time I have entered one of these restaurants:

What's in it for me?
What's in it for them?

I have not found a good answer to either one of these questions.

When customers enter a restaurant, they come with a certain set of expectations. They expect to be shown to a table. They expect to examine a menu and tell a waiter what items they want. They expect to have those items brought to them in some specific order. When customers enter a cafeteria restaurant, their expectations change slightly. They do not expect a menu. They expect to pick up a tray and move along a logically sequenced serving line, selecting items that appeal to them and adding these to their tray. Then they expect to go to a checkout point where a cashier will tally their purchases and collect their money. These are the paradigms.

Innovation breaks paradigms but it does so in ways that benefit the customer (or, at least, do not have a negative impact on the customer). The multi-station model that these chains use does not appear to me to have any benefit to the customer and, worse, to actually have a negative impact on him or her.

First, the customer becomes confused when entering the restaurant. The model is different and it is not immediately obvious what the new model is because the new model is actually pretty complex.

Second, the multiple stations actually add steps to the process. Instead of ordering food once, you order it at each station. Instead of one person tallying your purchase and collecting your payment, a tally is made at each station and then the tallies are consolidated and charged at a different location—the cashier's station.

I might be able to justify these costs imposed on the customer if there were some significant gain to the business. But I just don't see the gain to the business. The number of employees does not seem less. They are somewhat more specialized, so perhaps they are more efficient or can be trained at a lower cost, but these savings would not be great and I see no sign that the customer is gaining a lower cost as a result.

So, this just appears to be novelty to me. A Pet Rock Restaurant. I avoid both chains because, whatever reason they have for their innovative approach, it provides no benefit to me.

The Lost Baggage Problem

As noted in an earlier workout, flying is no fun and when you get to your final destination and wait an hour for baggage that never arrives, it can become agony.

In this workout, your task is to think through how baggage gets handled and list the steps you would use to:

1. Reduce the possibility of loss
2. Improve the speed and certainty of locating lost luggage when the first effort fails.

There is no sample answer here. The important learning for you will be the process of sitting back and working through the problem. A real world answer would take costs into account. We can not do that here so no sample answer would be helpful.

Where Do I Put My Glasses?

Note that the problem here is not finding where you absent-mindedly put your glasses. It is what to do with the glasses when you are not using them.

There are several solutions available, but none of them seem to work.

You can put the glasses in a shirt pocket, but not every outfit includes a shirt pocket.

You can hang them on a lanyard around your neck but lanyards are not all that attractive and the glasses themselves are exposed when carried this way and subject to damage.

I have a device with a pin like an earring post attached to a metal circle. I can pin that on my shirt and stick one of the earpieces through it. But I have a tendency to forget to remove this item from the shirt when I put it into the laundry.

Is there another way of handling this problem that achieves the goal of keeping your glasses handy without requiring some elaborate work on the owner's part?

Again, no sample answer is provided. You should judge for yourself whether your approach works and provides net utility.

Suggested Reading

There are a large number of books about innovation. They can be divided into several categories.

Some books are focused on business model innovation. That is, they discuss approaches to pricing, distribution channel, or the like. I have not included any of those books below though, since they do not necessarily reflect on product innovation. However, it is worth noting that innovation in business models typically leads to product innovation. When a company goes from delivering music on CDs to delivering music via download, more than the distribution channel changes.

Other books approach product innovation in different ways, most of which were at least touched on in this book. Many look at creating an innovative environment. Others reflect on developing individual innovation skills. Still others propose various methods for approaching innovation.

The list below includes books from all of these categories. Product innovation needs to encompass all three of these facets.

Clayton Christensen. Dr. Christensen is a prolific author and editor of innovation books and a professor at Harvard Business School. His books tend to focus on the big issues such as responding to disruptive technologies. All are insightful, interesting, and thought-provoking.

Among his most popular works are:

Seeing What's Next: Using Theories of Innovation to Predict Industry Change (Cambridge: Harvard Business School Press, 2004)

The Innovator's Dilemma: When New Technologies Cause Great Firms to Fail (New York: Collins, 2003)

Harvard Business Review on Innovation (Cambridge: Harvard Business School Press, 2001)

Elaine Dundon

The Seeds of Innovation (New York, AMACOM, 2002). This book covers three significant areas of product innovation:

1. Tools for stimulating ideas
2. Processes for selection of ideas
3. Organizational issues in innovation

Andrew Hargadon

How Breakthroughs Happen (Cambridge: Harvard Business School Press, 2003). This book is oriented toward case studies of innovations and draws from them a theory that innovation occurs through a collective activity during which old and new concepts are "captured" and combined to create innovative approaches.

Thomas Kelley

The Ten Faces of Innovation (New York, Doubleday Currency, 2001)
The Art of Innovation (New York: Doubleday Currency, 2005)

Kelley's books are among the best at dealing with personalities of innovators and creating an innovative environment. His anecdotes are enjoyable and enlightening, and his writing style is very entertaining.

Michel Robert

Product Innovation Strategy, Pure and Simple: How Winning Companies Outpace Their Competitors (New York: McGraw-Hill, 1995). This is a classic book that focuses on the innovation process.

Evan Schwartz

Juice (Cambridge: Harvard Business School Press, 2004). This book looks at creative minds and moments of great creative breakthroughs. It is personality-focused and provides real insight into how these moments happen and the people they happen to. It will not tell you how to create innovative products, but it will motivate you to do so.

Anthony Ulwick

What Customers Want: Using Outcome-Driven Innovation to Create Breakthrough Products and Services (New York: McGraw-Hill, 2005). A strong and clear approach to creating a process for product innovation.

Craig Vogel

The Design of Things to Come (Boston: Wharton School Publishing, 2005). Vogel spends a fair amount of space on "pragmatic innovation" and recognizes the core concept that utility is a driving force in product innovation.

Notes

Part 1

1. When the word *product* is used in this book, it generally includes services within its meaning, as opposed to being limited to "hard" products. Chapter 8 will put particular focus on the use of the methods in this book for services.
2. Services are always utilitarian. As will be discussed in Chapter 8, services (even when their ultimate object is aesthetic, such as a beauty treatment) are simply the substitution of someone else's efforts for ours. Services save us work, and so they are useful.

Chapter 1

1. "The World's Most Innovative Companies," *Business Week,* April 24, 2006, p. 63.

2. W. Chan Kim and Renee Mauborgne, "Value Innovation: The Strategic Logic of High Growth," *Harvard Business Review*, January 1997, pp. 102–112.
3. Larry Huston and Nabil Sakkab, "Connect and Develop." *Harvard Business Review,* March 2006, p. 58.
4. http://www.apple.com/pr/library/2006/jan/18results.html.
5. DISConnect, www.houstonpress.com /2007–01–04/news/disconnect/.

Chapter 2

1. See http://www.contractormag.com/articles/newsarticle.cfm?news id = 677.
2. For the compulsively empirical, here are several sources that discuss the faucet market in general along with specific efforts at innovation in the faucet industry: www.usatoday.com/money/industries/retail/2005–05–03-ffaucetsex.htm; Kenneth Helm, "Strategy: Moen Taps Into Elegance to Dampen Competition," *Media Week,* March 21, 2005; www.Nucifora.com/art_193.html.
3. www.moen.com.
4. www.deltafaucet.com.
5. Will Hermes, "Music: Springsteen's Take on Classic Folk," *New York Times*, April 16, 2006, Sec. 2, p. 22.

Chapter 3

1. Actually it turned out that the father of Henry II of England was not the son of Henry I, so my thinking was entirely wrong.
2. This innovation was made possible by a disruptive advance in technology. That is often the case, but it does not diminish the fact that

an innovator needs to grasp the impact of the technology on the customer's life and take advantage of that advance in technology.

Chapter 4

1. Bill Vlasic, "Changing Minds: What Detroit Can Do to Win Back Car Buyers," Detroit News, Jan. 3, 2007, www.detroitnews.com/apps/ pbcs.dll/article? AID = 20070103/AUTO01/701030382.

Chapter 5

1. I did a search for a similar product on the Internet and did not find one. That failure raises two possibilities: (1) There is a chance to get rich here, or (2) this is a really bad idea that has been tried and found wanting.

Chapter 7

1. http://www.simonsays.com/content/book.cfm?tab = 1& pid = 409492&agid = 2 .
2. This raises an interesting question. 3M produces both Scotch tape and Post-it notes. Did the success of the latter cannibalize the sales of the former? The roll of tape on my desk has not been changed in a year and is barely down from its original size. But I have gone through several packs of Post-it notes in that time.

3. Roland T. Rust, Debora Viana Thompson, and Rebecca W. Hamilton, "Defeating Feature Fatigue," *Harvard Business Review*, February 2006, p. 98.
4. This is the phenomenon behind the famous Schrodinger's cat experiment in quantum physics. The mere fact of observation changes the outcome of the experiment. http://whatis.techtarget.com/definition/0,,sid9_gci341236,00.html.

Chapter 8

1. It is true that in some markets there are "buyer's" agents, but when your pay depends upon your selling as many houses as you can, the notion that you are representing the buyer is a difficult one to defend.
2. In Appendix B, there is an innovation workout involving a much less complex portion of the services industry, dry cleaning, and these more unified services do present simpler problems, like those we have discussed earlier.

Appendix B

1. Even there, I have a question about net utility. Is this fitted sheet actually a productivity gain when folding it for storage is a more complex task than folding a flat sheet and when those elastic corners never really seem to stay in place for long?
2. See www.firstsearch.com.
3. There actually were two people sitting there, the finance person and the salesperson.

About the Author

Denis Hauptly is Vice President for Technology Strategy at Thomson Global Resources, a division of the Thomson Corporation in Zug, Switzerland. He has previously served as Vice President, New Product Development, at Thomson West; Vice President, Content, at Thomson Global Resources AG in Switzerland; and Vice President, Technology Product Development, at Thomson West.

Prior to joining The Thomson Corporation in 1994, Mr. Hauptly served in a variety of positions in the Federal Courts and the United States Department of Justice, including Special Master for the United States Court of Federal Claims and Director of Judicial Education for the Federal Courts.

He is the author of four books and numerous articles on history and law. His books have been awarded an ALA

Notable Book designation, and he is the recipient of the Benjamin Franklin Award for Best Writing on the Constitution. A native of New Jersey, he is a graduate of St. Michael's College in American Studies and has a law degree from the University of Notre Dame.

He is married to Kay Knapp and they reside in Thalwil, Switzerland, and Minneapolis, Minnesota.

Index

parking the car innovation workout, 116, 192

passion
  as hiring criterion, 169
  in innovators, 157
  in true believers, 161–162

peer groups, 171–172

peer review, 49

people, *see* innovators

people skills, 156, 159

perception, of customers, 16–18, 142

Pet Rocks, 6–7

picture hanging, 77–79, 82–87
  building of device for, 185
  eliminating steps from, 84–85
  labor-saving device for, 85–87, 180–183
  sales and marketing of device for, 187–188
  sources of pain in, 77
  steps in, 77–79
  "sweet spot" steps in, 82–84

pilot testing, 50

planning
  culture of innovation in, 96
  driven out by implementation, 91–92
  revenue goals in, 92–93

Plasmacluster ionizer, 55

Post-it notes, 106

pragmatism
  in big innovators, 159
  as hiring criterion, 169
  as innovation skill, 157

premium level of commodities, 15–16

process-driven innovation, 89–95

culture of innovation combined with, 98

culture of innovation vs., 89, 95–98

innovation goals in, 92–93

lowest common denominator level in, 93–94

and management objectives, 90–92

Procter & Gamble, 14, 92, 97

product approval, 179–184
  in innovation plan, 149
  presentation to management in, 180–184

product building, 184–186

product launches, 179–180

product ratings, 146–147

products
  building, 184–186
  customers' actual uses of, 139–141
  expense in creating, 179
  matching task and, 141–144
  net utility validation of concepts for, 145–147
  and ownership of innovations, 173–175
  usability vs. abilities of, 107–108

propane barbecue grills, 74

prototyping, 47, 182

publication of ideas, 49

Purina, 141

questioning skill
  in big innovators, 159
  as hiring criterion, 169
  as innovation skill, 157

questions
  for corporate alignment, 178
  making assumptions about, 39, 40